Advan

"We have known of Dr. Cindy Bigbie's work for some years. We never knew how truly impactful it was until March 28, 2010. That was the day our son, Conor, shot his fiancée, Ann. Nonviolent Communication (NVC) was introduced to Conor by Cindy in a prison betterment program. Since then, Conor has stated that if he had been taught NVC while in high school, he would not be in prison and Ann would be alive. This real-world example shows the profound impact Cindy's work could have on a community. Everyone, everywhere, can benefit from learning the skills associated with NVC. We recommend, from the hearts of two who know, that you read this book and learn Dr. Cindy Bigbie's Method."

–JULIE AND MICHAEL MCBRIDE,
President of Florida Restorative Justice Association

"Our most highly rated and sought-after curriculum is the one that Dr. Bigbie brought to Thomas University years ago. It was all based on the very same processes that she puts forth in this writing. I have seen enormous changes in how teachers respond in critical communication instances due to Dr. Bigbie's legacy at Thomas University."

–SUSAN LYNN, PhD,
Chair and Professor, Thomas University Division of Education

"Cindy and I have been close colleagues and friends for many years in the world of Nonviolent Communication (NVC). She is the real deal—a depth of dedication and commitment to human healing and transformation I have found stunning and awe-inspiring since first knowing her. This very personal story of her mother, their relationship, and healing trauma in her family gives us an up-close, intimate experience of how this kind of transformation can really happen. Told in rich, moving, and poetic language, this story is a profound offering and inspiration to all of us individually and also collectively on our human journey of healing and transformation of violence and suffering."

–JOHN KINYON,
Co-creator of the international Mediate Your Life training,
trainer of the Center for Nonviolent Communication (CNVC)

"From the very beginning of this beautifully written book, Dr. Bigbie plants within us a heightened awareness of the role intergenerational trauma plays in our human conduct and experience. This very personal story of her life not only sheds light on the mysteries of life and death, but also shows us the path to end the vicious cycle of violence. This is a courageous, moving, and deeply personal story that will change your life."

–HEART PHOENIX,
Chair and Co-Founder of The River Phoenix Center for Peacebuilding

"After more than twenty years educating students who have experienced significant trauma, what I have gained from Cindy and The Bigbie Method has reformed my thinking and provided a framework for connection and empathy. As the principal of our district's alternative school, I see daily examples of the effectiveness of The Bigbie Method on my campus, as students with limited awareness of effective communication are learning to give and receive empathy. If you open your mind and your soul to what is offered in this book, relationships will be restored, and stronger communities will be built."

–AMY ALVIS,
Principal, Second Chance and Success Academy

"Dr. Cindy Bigbie has gained widespread recognition as a restorative practices director, as an entrepreneur, as a podcaster, and for her innovative Nonviolent Communication course. Moreover, she has inspired our community to find transformational connection and healing. Her inspirational reach now continues with her story of intergenerational trauma and the path to healing."

–JEREMIAH W. MURPHY,
President of Connection First and Professor of Physics
at Florida State University

"After spending years in the advocacy space to end gun violence in our country, I grew increasingly dismayed by the entrenched and seemingly intractable conflict between otherwise reasonable and caring Americans. I was seeking another way to approach the issue that would align with my faith and core values of kindness, compassion, and respect for all people, so I signed up for an NVC (Nonviolent Communication) course with Dr. B. This learning has not only invigorated my advocacy and professional worlds, it has transformed my most treasured and intimate relationships with family and friends. Our hurting world desperately needs caring communities skilled in giving and receiving empathy, and Dr. B is just the one to show us the way."

–KATE KILE,
volunteer and former leader with Moms Demand Action for
Gun Sense in America and leader with Capital Area Justice Ministry–
Gun Violence Strategy Team

"Part textbook, part personal memoir, Bigbie's book offers us a critical grounding in Nonviolent Communication through an intimate account of its stunning application in her own life and activism. A necessary read for community organizers, educators, and anyone who lives with, works alongside, or creates with others, this book teaches how to heal through relationship the sensitive parts of growing up and the tender stories that stay with us. This is one you'll hope your loved ones will read."

–HANNAH SCHWADRON, MFA, PhD,
Associate Professor of Dance at Florida State University
and Community Connections volunteer

"Cindy beautifully illustrates how trauma, both individually and within families, can be healed and transformed into something beautiful and meaningful when it is processed through Nonviolent Communication. This transformation and the skillful use of nonviolent communication can be a way for us to have peace and love within our hearts and thereby spread that peace and love to heal those around us and the world."

–ANGEL EASON,
attorney at Legal Services of North Florida, striving toward fairness and justice for everyone, and a long-time student of Cindy Bigbie and NVC

"Cindy Bigbie (of The Bigbie Method) offers us unprecedented guidance to break through the fear and pain that fuel tension and separation in our relationships. Cindy's teaching prioritizes self-responsibility and reflection, enabling us to become more deeply aware of our own capacity for love and empathy. From a place of compassion, she helps us learn to move toward each other, even when we feel scared and hurt, so that we can transform our relationships and heal our communities."

–KATHLEEN MCGOEY,
President of KMA, Inc., former Executive Director of
Longmont Community Justice Partnership

"Cindy is a pioneer of brave and caring heart-centered communication strategies. Working with her, serving teens and their families for nearly five years, I was consistently awed by what I saw as profound purpose and courage. Her devotion and skill are so palpable that it was common for clients to have deeply moving, tearful breakthroughs within thirty minutes of meeting her (to say nothing of her sweet, connecting humor!)."

–DAN KAHN,
Executive Director of the Florida Restorative Justice Association

"The Bigbie Method is an accessible, trauma-responsive approach to resolving conflict and harm while staying connected with the people in our lives. Dr. Bigbie has found a way to create a space vast enough to hold people's pain, deepen self-connection, and foster authentic relational repair. Using this approach to communication not only heals internal wounds, it invites love to enliven all of our relationships."

–DR. SHEILA MCMAHON,
Professor of Social Work at Barry University

"Dr. Bigbie, my Nonviolent Communication teacher, shines her genuine light and elevates your consciousness to know a way to peace, to ahimsa, to connection, to healing. Dr. Bigbie's authentic voice touches my soul, and I know that you, too, will feel connected to her words and her spirit. Her integrity and compassion jump from the pages she writes straight to your heart. I feel deep gratitude for the way Dr. Bigbie has changed my life and taught me the ways of Nonviolent Communication, a way not only to create peace, but to be peace. I am so excited for all of us to share in her wisdom and grow together in healing and love."

–MELISSA GREEN,
Broward Hope Court/RJ Director

"It's all about connection: connection to the past and present. Connection regained and renewed to create pathways to healing from trauma and establishing new beginnings. Dr. Bigbie sets the power of connection within the context of healing and moving forward on this journey through trauma and pain to renewal and healing. Dr. Bigbie tells this story with compassion and humility so her mother's legacy can be used to change the trajectories of everyone who reads it, and this story can change the world."

–DR. SCOTTYE CASH,
Professor of Social Work, Ohio State University

"Dr. Cindy Bigbie is the true champion of Restorative Justice and Nonviolent Communication. Her work and knowledge help in the most difficult situations and truly lead to effective problem-solving and growth. Her tried-and-true methods make a significant impact in the lives of so many at-risk youth and show them that there's a path of hope and healing for their lives. She is a true trailblazer and leader in breaking down barriers and helping people through some of the most traumatic experiences. We're all better friends, parents, partners, and neighbors because of Cindy and her lessons. This book should be required reading in every courthouse in America!"

–JESSICA YEARY,
Public Defender for Florida's Second Judicial Circuit

MY LINK TO MILDRED

MY LINK TO MILDRED

INTERRUPTING THE EPIDEMIC OF TRAUMA
VIA NONVIOLENT COMMUNICATION

DR. CINDY BIGBIE

HOUNDSTOOTH
PRESS

My Link to Mildred

Interrupting the Epidemic of Trauma via Nonviolent Communication

FIRST EDITION

ISBN 978-1-5445-4254-6 Hardcover
      978-1-5445-4255-3 Paperback
      978-1-5445-4256-0 Ebook

To my mommy—

Marci Landis

9/12/41 – 5/5/22

Our Lesson on Love!

Contents

Introduction

"Will you hold onto their stories and write another chapter?
Or will you throw the book away and write anew?"

—EPIPHANY

My mother died, last week, just five days ago to be exact—in the
room right next to me, my TV room. Her things are still around.
The soap in my bathroom is soap that washed her face and hands.
It's all very surreal, this new existence. My brother, sister, husband,
and brother-in-law were all there holding her after she took her last
breath. The very same breath that birthed me into existence. The
same breath that breathed in me until the chord was cut and I took
in air on my own. In the Jewish faith, there is a prayer that I love so
much: "Sh'ma Yisrael Adonei Elohenu Adonei Echad. The Lord
our God, the Lord is One!" My daughter sang it at the intimate
funeral we had graveside the day after she died. And somehow, I now
understand viscerally its meaning more than ever. This idea of her
living in me. It's not just a "nice" or "comforting" concept, it's real.

Yesterday, I visited her gravesite early in the morning. I brought
my yoga mat, a candle, some Palo Santo, and a poem I had written
that she requested, several months ago, I give her for Mother's Day.

Yes, it was Mother's Day—just three days after her passing. I was scared, waking up and then driving to the cemetery, wondering how it would be to be with her alone, at dawn, she in her new state— buried beneath the earth. I was scared I would be frightened or sick to my stomach, or the kind of sad that hurts so deeply you think you, yourself, might die. But I experienced none of those things. The cemetery was holy and beautiful. Old trees everywhere and bird song, morning light and quiet. My body, mind, and spirit felt a surprising and joyful peace with a mixture of extreme tenderness and gratitude. I almost went down the road of "What is wrong with me? My mother died and I feel so good, a peace like never before." And then I realized that, by her voice being inside me, she would want it this way. My oneness with her and all of life would want to be known and celebrated.

When someone we love dies, I think we hope for a sign from them. Something from beyond to hold them to us, to let us know there is more than this world. A week or so before she died, I, playfully, suggested we come up with a sign she could give me. She was worried that she might not be able to follow through, not knowing how things actually work after we leave this plane. So, I abandoned that idea with little attachment. However, my mama did not fail me. In fact, her sign came yesterday. On Mother's Day.

A few close people to me know how during the last few springs— when the world is coming to life with new growth, splendid colors, beauty—I've been pissed. I literally would experience a pain in my heart due to dogwood trees. Let me explain. I live in Tallahassee, Florida. It's a beautiful, breathtaking city, in my opinion. And spring with its bright green growth, pink azaleas, and dotted white dogwoods—the contrast everywhere—was like food for my soul. I'd almost jump out of my body with joy just driving around this darn city. And then, about five years ago, I started to slowly notice something was missing. The dots of white—where were they? It wasn't until about a year after the disease began, that someone shared we had a blight that had wiped out all the dogwoods in our beautiful city. It was like a death to me, but worse, a death that no one seemed to notice or care about or even mention. Each spring, thereafter, I'd drive around kind of crazy with anger about the dogwoods. Spring was not the same and no one cared. Was I the only one that mourned? I even wrote a poem about it. My heart actually hurt! Last spring, I noticed that the pain had lessened some. I didn't feel as angry but still thought about the missing trees. And this spring that just passed, well, it didn't exist at all because I spent the entire month of April at Tallahassee Memorial Hospital at my dying mother's bedside. No time to think about the dogwoods. I reminded myself there would be other springs and was grateful to abandon the season, temporarily, and spend complete and precious presence with the woman who birthed me—and who gave me the signal after all.

Picture this. Yoga mat rolled out toward the mound of dirt under which her body lay. I placed the candle right on top with a couple of special stones that I call my "safety stones." Mother's Day, alone in the cemetery early morning. Me, standing in prayer pose, bare feet, on my mat. I hear a bird call, something I don't recognize. It's calling over and over and over. Clearly, wanting my attention. It's a red-headed woodpecker (a symbol of change, passing, opportunity) diagonally across from my mom's new home. And it calls to me over and over. Poignantly, trying to tell me something. And then I see it. I realize this stunning bird is calling me from—yes—a big, beautiful dogwood tree. Literally, the only one I know of in this whole darn city. Thank you, mama, for that gift, that sign of hope and beauty. Spring, and all its potential, is more alive than ever, thanks to your death. I understand now, at least a tad more, how life and death morph into one thing and how you are not lost at all. You truly live in me, and your story and message live through me. So much beauty, even in loss. And I feel peace, even on Mother's Day, days after you left us.

As she was dying, my mother told me (she didn't really ask) to write her story, and I promised I would. In fact, the title of this book, I've kept for years. I knew I would write it even before she asked. I've been gifted with the unusual ability to string things together. So, while this is a story of my mother's trauma, it's also a story of humanity's trauma and how to break the cycle of trauma which, I believe, is epidemic and the root cause of all the violence we see perpetuated in our world. This is my mother's gift to humanity. The metamorphosis of her family's historical trauma into something that has the potential to make the world more peaceful for many. I pray I do her story justice and that I can explain her story, its link to trauma, and all our trauma, in a way that helps to turn the tide on the violence in our world.

Please note that throughout this book, I occasionally put words in quotes. In Nonviolent Communication (NVC), we strive to use language "free of judgment," meaning that words state what is seen, heard, or felt (by touch) and indicate needs met or not. Sometimes it's just easier and shorter to use a word or statement that doesn't fit that template. In many cases, I have used quotes around the word or phrase to retain my integrity and to at least acknowledge when I choose to use "judgmental" language.

CHAPTER 1

THE EPIDEMIC OF TRAUMA

"Imagine, if you will, a disease—one that has only subtle outward symptoms but can hijack your entire body without notice; one that transfers easily between parent and child, one that can last a lifetime (even lifetimes) if untreated."

—DR. PAUL CONTI

Sometime around 2004, because of my heartbreak about George Bush Jr. being elected for a second term, I became the local representative for the United States Department of Peace campaign. I remember President Bush saying something along the lines of his presidency being ordained by God. Now, in hindsight, I can see the workings of divinity in my own life and the evolution of events because of his re-election. He was right; God works in strange ways.

I'm fortunate to live in a neighborhood where my children ran free and played "Ghost and Graveyard" at dark with their neighborhood friends. Most of the people living here moved in around the same time, and we had kids the same ages. We would have Friday happy hours, and on Sunday afternoons, Mr. Rusty would often host football on his front lawn. It was adorable seeing all these different-sized and -aged kids playing together. Get this, we even had hot air balloons that would often land in our community early Saturday or Sunday mornings, and the kids would come running from all different streets to watch them land. Ridiculously picturesque, I know! I love my neighbors. When you live next door to people, you know them in the everyday way. You know them by their willingness to help you build your deck, loan you sugar, share the plants in their yards. When my mother died, their kindness and support came in many forms.

ENTER THE
DEPARTMENT OF PEACE

So, years ago, when George Bush Jr. was re-elected and I knew most of my neighbors had helped that happen, I was devastated and beyond confused. How could these people that I love so deeply, with whom I have such sweet history, think so differently from me? It's a long story that I won't go into here, but I decided to join the campaign for a United States Department of Peace (DOP) because I wanted to work toward a vision of what was possible, and I was tired of fighting against what I didn't want. I was seeking understanding and a way to contribute to what I saw as a disconnected and disintegrating world.

I had never done anything actively political before. As the DOP district rep, my job was to help get the word out and educate folks, locally, about the campaign. In that vein, I would table at community events, meet with City and County Commissioners, and host meetings in my home to gain local support. (Figure 1 shows a picture of my daughters, Tylre and Jesse, signing people in as they came to my home for a DOP meeting.) My goal was to get many people locally to understand and support the legislation and even get our city to sign a resolution in support of the bill. I got many people on board and even brought a large contingency to Washington, DC, for the National Department of Peace Conference, after which we went to Capitol Hill and lobbied our Senators and Representatives for a U.S. Department of Peace (DOP). That was an eye-opening experience, to see how the doors of our Representatives are literally open to citizens bold enough to come knocking (Figures 2 and 3).

Figure 1: Daughters signing in people for DOP meeting

Figure 2: Daughter, Jesse, meeting with Congressman Boyd about DOP

Figure 3: Marching at Capitol Hill

ENTER NONVIOLENT COMMUNICATION

The idea behind the DOP was birthed by a relatively recent body of knowledge on research-based programs and processes to help bring people together, especially in conflict. Those who created the Bill believed these programs/processes could be helpful at a domestic and international level to interrupt violence. This department could work together with the Department of Defense to help reroute conflicts of all kinds. I first learned about Nonviolent Communication (NVC) through the DOP effort where national leaders had collaborated with the Center for Nonviolent Communication to teach those of us in the field how to "Be the Bill" we were promoting. In other words, in the 1960s, when so many people were advocating for peace, they often, and ironically, resorted to fighting to promote peace. DOP leaders wanted us to go about this differently. They wanted us to model the very processes we were promoting. Enter NVC!

We used to get on conference calls when they were a new thing. Hundreds of people from across the country were trained on these calls from one of NVC's finest trainers, Miki Kashtan. I was smitten from the beginning. I understood the potential of this process and also knew I could not gain the skills overnight. It was a lifelong journey. And journey it has been! The purpose of this book is to educate the masses on the epidemic of trauma, to educate people on NVC, and to help everyone understand how NVC has the potential for healing and halting the cycle of trauma that is passed on from one generation to the next.

A SEA OF PAIN

In addition to NVC, the other gift that the DOP work brought me was my experience with the Challenge Days program. Somewhere amid trying to get my city to sign a resolution in support of the DOP, I adopted the tactic of letting my community experience, firsthand, some of the programs that a DOP could promote. I don't recall how many Challenge Days I volunteered for before I approached my own city and school district to bring it here, but it was quite a few, and I experienced this program in schools of all types: majority minority, majority white, wealthy, poor. My experience was the same each time—our epidemic of trauma was on display. In 2008, I got our school district, city, and private donors to fund two Challenge Days at Rickards High School. Since then, almost daily, I replay a picture of that Rickards gym during Challenge Days; the image haunts and motivates me deeply.

The mission of Challenge Days is "to create a world where every person in our communities feels safe, loved, and celebrated." Roughly one hundred students and twenty-five adults (from the school and the extended community) come together and get to really know one another. It's based on the premise that people are like icebergs; we show only a little of our true selves while most of who we are is kept "under the water." We've learned to do this to keep one another safe and, ironically, it has the opposite effect. We become more distant and able to hurt one another easier. For one special day—with games, music, dancing, and sharing—Challenge Days helps people reveal what is under their water line and build a magical and safer school community.

After playing and dancing, the program moves into a bit more solemnity, and the program leaders share their stories, which are jaw-dropping, usually about horrific abuse and loss. By sharing them, they model how vulnerability allows for greater connection and respect, and they set up an activity called "If You Really Knew Me!" It is the image of this activity that has lived within me daily for the past fourteen years.

This is how the activity goes. After sharing, the leaders ask participants to do the same. Groups of four students and one adult circle up around the gym. Each person in the circle is given one minute to share, starting with "If you really knew me…"

Each time I have participated in this activity, it is astonishing what comes out in those five minutes. Stories of homelessness, hunger, abuse, loneliness, loss... over and over and over. Looking across Rickards gym, small circles of young people finally getting to share their truth—it was a sea of pain! It doesn't matter what kind of a school; this scenario plays itself out in the exact same way. Our children and our world are suffering from epidemic trauma in its various forms and, instead of learning how to reroute it, we have learned to cover it up. But there was that picture, a sea of circles, each one sharing a sigh of relief and a bucket of tears, as children finally told their stories, their trauma.

That was 2008, twelve years after the landmark study of Adverse Childhood Experiences (ACE) was first published. But it has taken years for that research to begin to have inroads into our systems. Let's talk about that here and about trauma in general. I want to help individuals connect the dots between what I saw in that gym during Challenge Days—the cycle of generational trauma—and how it shows up in the violence and disconnection we see in our schools and our society as a whole.

WHAT IS TRAUMA?

When I Google "What is trauma?" there are some common themes that occur across sites.

- ► It is defined more by a person's response to an event or circumstances than the event/circumstances themselves.

Trauma is not the thing that happens to a person; it is the person's response to the event, the way the brain reacts.

► It is caused by deeply distressing or disturbing events/circumstances that overwhelm an individual's ability to cope.

► Trauma diminishes an individual's sense of self and their ability to feel a full range of emotions and experiences.

► Trauma does not discriminate, and it is pervasive throughout the world.

► Trauma typically occurs because of circumstances that involve the loss of control, betrayal, abuse of power, helplessness, pain, confusion, and/or loss. The event need not rise to the level of war, natural disaster, or personal assault to affect a person profoundly and alter their experiences.

Because trauma reactions fall across a wide spectrum, psychologists have developed categories to differentiate between types of traumas.

Complex Trauma happens repeatedly. It often results in direct harm, emotional or physical, to the individual. The effects of complex trauma accumulate over time. The traumatic experience often transpires within a certain period or within a specific relationship, and often in a particular place or setting.

Post-Traumatic Stress Disorder (PTSD) can develop after a person has been exposed to a terrifying event or has been through an ordeal in which intense physical harm occurred or was threatened. Sufferers of this PTSD have persistent and frightening thoughts and memories of their ordeal.

Developmental Trauma Disorder is a recent term in the study of psychology. This condition forms during a child's first three years of life. The result of abuse, neglect, and/or abandonment, developmental trauma affects the infant or child's neurological, cognitive, and psychological development. It interrupts the child's ability to attach to an adult caregiver.

An adult who inflicts this kind of harm doesn't usually do it intentionally. Rather, it happens because they are unaware of the social and emotional needs of children. And, we will learn, these individuals have often experienced trauma themselves and are reacting, unconsciously, with their own trauma response.

Specific experiences that may be traumatic include:

- ▶ Physical, sexual, and emotional abuse
- ▶ Childhood neglect
- ▶ Living with a family member with mental health or substance use disorders
- ▶ Sudden, unexplained separation from a loved one
- ▶ Poverty
- ▶ Racism, discrimination, and oppression
- ▶ Violence in the community, war, or terrorism

Although trauma can occur at any age, it has particularly debilitating long-term effects on children's developing brains. Often referred to as adverse childhood experiences (ACEs), exposure to these experiences in childhood is common across all sectors of society. The Adverse Childhood Experiences Study, first published in 1998, found 62 percent of US adults have at least one ACE, and 25 percent of US adults have three or more. The ACE research also revealed the devastating impact of these experiences. The research confirms what I saw in the Rickards gym in 2008. Trauma is epidemic!

Regardless of the type of trauma, there are some common symptoms that may be expected to occur after a traumatic event or circumstance. Most of these symptoms are, in fact, the brain's natural response to helping the individual survive and/or make sense of the world. They often continue throughout a person's life, years after the actual event or circumstance. The following are some common reactions:

- **Intrusive thoughts and memories:** After a traumatic event or circumstance, it is common to experience some intrusive thoughts and memories of the traumatic event. This is especially likely to occur when you encounter something (for example, a person, place, or image) that reminds you of the traumatic events.

- **Hypervigilance:** It is also very natural to feel more on guard and aware of your surroundings after a traumatic event or circumstance. This is actually a very protective symptom as your body is attempting to keep you safe by making you more aware of potential sources of threat and danger. This built-in safety mechanism is going to be more sensitive following a traumatic event or circumstance due to the brain's automatic response to keeping one safe.

► **Hyperarousal:** Just as you are going to likely be more on guard, you are also likely going to feel more keyed up and on edge following a traumatic event or circumstance. This is, again, part of your body's natural protection system. Fear and anxiety tell us that there is danger present, and all the bodily sensations that go along with fear and anxiety are essentially designed to help us respond to that danger. They are preparing us to fight, flee, or freeze. Following a traumatic event or circumstance, your body's alarm system is going to be more sensitive to protect you from future traumatic events.

► **Perceived lack of safety:** After a traumatic event or circumstance, our assumptions about the world being a safe and secure place are understandably shattered. Consequently, people may think that any situation or place is potentially dangerous. Places or situations you once felt secure in may now feel stressful or scary and be anxiety-provoking. This is especially likely to occur in situations or places that remind you of your traumatic events.

► **Unconscious, destructive self-talk:** The brain's default mode network (DMN) is programmed to recall things that were said or done to a person at a young age, and our unconscious self-talk can mimic what we heard about ourselves as a child.

All these changes occur because of the way our brain responds and adjusts to traumatic events/circumstances. To help the reader thread together why we have an epidemic of trauma, how our histories are literally passed down to one another, and the epidemic of violence and disconnection we experience in the world, it's important to provide insight into how the brain deals with trauma.

HOW THE BRAIN DEALS WITH TRAUMA

The brain has so many functions, but one of the most important things it does is to keep us safe. As we experience life and take in information from the world, our brain houses this information in memories largely for the purpose of helping us move through life with more ease and safety. Our memories help us determine the activities we should keep doing because they produce "good" results, and which things we might want to avoid because of negative consequences. When processing traumatic events, our brains go into overdrive to keep us safe. In fact, the brain will continue to use the blueprints of the past even after the danger has passed or the trauma event has ceased. Literally, the trauma event changes the way the brain operates. It does this by activating the amygdala, shrinking the hippocampus, and decreasing the prefrontal cortex. Let's go into that next.

Traumatic Stress Activates the Amygdala

This almond-shaped structure is found in the part of the brain called the limbic system, and its primary function is to process emotions and memories associated with fear and pleasure. The amygdala is connected to many other parts of the brain structures and organizes physiological responses (like breathing) based on cognitive information. So, if the amygdala is stimulated by a perceived threat, it will send information to the body to get ready to face that threat or to move away from it (fight, flight, freeze.) Once the threat is over, the frontal lobes or higher-level parts of the brain will come online to bring the body system back into homeostasis. For someone who has experienced trauma, however, the amygdala often stays activated, and the body systems associated with that fight, flight, freeze response stay in motion or are quick to activate. The amygdala has a hard time determining a present threat versus residual threats from the past, causing the traumatized person to be on heightened alert and on edge often. When reminded of a traumatic event/experience in any way, the brain and body will respond just as if the actual event were occurring in real time. An overactive amygdala can cause dysfunction, such as chronic stress, heightened fear, increased irritation, an inability to calm down, and insomnia.

Traumatic Stress Can Shrink the Hippocampus

The hippocampus, which is located near the amygdala, is responsible for storing and retrieving our memories and for helping us discern between what happened in the past and what is occurring in the present. Research shows that high levels of stress on the body can result in the shrinking of the hippocampus. So, basically, the hippocampus does not have as much volume to house memories and therefore compensates by keeping old, traumatic memories at the forefront of our minds, causing us to live in a constant state of strong reactivity.

When the hippocampus shrinks, it may become more difficult for your brain to hold onto memories. But here's where things get complicated: trauma-related stress deceives the hippocampus into thinking that memories related to anxiety are necessary to store and remember. So, the few memories you do hold onto will be those related to stress. In other words, trauma stress often wires your brain to remember failure, threat, and danger. Happier memories —such as those of success, achievement, and safety—are buried or lost entirely.

Trauma Stress Can Decrease Functions in the Prefrontal Cortex (PFC)

The PFC is part of the frontal lobe of the brain and makes up a large proportion of the entire brain. It is involved in several functions but is mostly known for the executive functions, meaning things such as self-control, planning, decision-making, and problem-solving. Scientific data shows that traumatic stress can diminish functionality in the prefrontal cortex. This can negatively impact our ability to learn new information, manage our emotions well, and deal with problems. In other words, traumatic stress can make logical thinking difficult which, in turn, can make individuals believe they are incapable of controlling their fear, anxiety, and other difficult emotions.

A SYMPHONY OF DYSFUNCTION

Living with traumatic stress can change the brain so much that daily life can be a challenge. High levels of stress hormones coupled with an overactive amygdala, a shrunken hippocampus, and a less active prefrontal cortex can cause:

- ▶ Anxiety
- ▶ Insomnia
- ▶ Irritability
- ▶ Flashbacks
- ▶ Nightmares
- ▶ Panic attacks
- ▶ Memory issues
- ▶ Poor concentration
- ▶ Trouble making decisions
- ▶ Difficulty learning new things

Fatigue and exhaustion are also common for people experiencing traumatic stress because the body is working overtime to protect the individual from perceived threats. All of this has an enormous impact on daily responsibilities, self-care, and our relationships.

Living with a brain that is always on alert can have a debilitating impact on one's interactions and relationships. When we are on heightened alert, we can easily misread cues and comments from the people around us. This can feed communication issues and put a tremendous strain on the connection we have with the people in all areas of our lives.

THE DEFAULT MODE NETWORK (DMN)

Earlier I mentioned the default mode network (DMN). The DMN is a group of brain regions that seem to show lower levels of activity when we are engaged in a particular task, such as paying attention, but higher levels of activity when we are awake and not involved in any specific mental exercise. When our brain is not attending to a specific task, it is often swept away with just thinking. During this "thinking time," and often without conscious awareness, we tend to daydream, recollect memories, imagine the future, monitor our surroundings, wonder about the intentions of others, and so on. Individuals who have experienced trauma, especially during their formative years, will draw upon the negative memories from that trauma, and develop a destructive DMN. This means the thoughts that go on in their mind when not engaged in an externally focused event will often be unconsciously negative about self and/or others. This damaging DMN is key in keeping the brain's system stuck in fight, flight, freeze. In her book *Your Resonant Self* (which I highly recommend), Sarah Peyton explains, "As our lives continue past the point of trauma, the amygdala is no longer reacting to real threats; rather, it is reacting *to internal voices* and perceiving them as threats, which is part of the looping stress of the DMN" (italics mine). This is why interactions and communications can quickly turn into misunderstandings and deep conflicts, which further feed the cycle.

All this information about trauma and its impact on the brain and, subsequently, our lives and interactions are further complicated when we learn that trauma is passed down through generations in multiple ways. As we have been discussing, trauma is behaviorally transmitted, with the trauma response occurring because of environmental events and/or circumstances. However, recent research has found that trauma response can also occur because of our genetic inheritance. Epigenetics is the study of what influences gene expression and how, and it is crucial to understanding the intergenerational effects of traumatic experiences. Currently, there is a whole area of science devoted to understanding epigenetics.

It's quite difficult to trace and study the gene pool and connected behaviors of individuals through generations; thus, scientists have resorted to animal studies to learn more about intergenerational trauma and its genetic impact. In 2014, researchers from Emory University found evidence of an intergenerational epigenetic pathway that seems to run through sperm. Working with mice, they paired a mild electric shock with the scent of a cherry blossom— every time the mice would smell the scent, they would receive the shock. This pairing eventually created a fear response to the odor that was accompanied with epigenetic alterations in the brain and sperm. Additionally, the offspring of these mice also showed evidence of fear related to the cherry scent, and they had the same epigenetic changes in their brains and sperm. What is crazy about this is that the offspring were never given the shock with the scent.

In fact, these effects carried over for two generations of the mice. The fear of the grandfather mouse was carried over to his sons and his grandsons, behaviorally and genetically. There is also evidence that this kind of intergenerational trauma occurs in humans. While studying the offspring of survivors of relatively recent tragedies such as 9/11, the Holocaust, and Vietnam, scientists document similar findings.

This piece from Resmaa Menakem's book *My Grandmother's Hands* does a great job of summarizing what is known thus far:

> The transference of trauma isn't just about how human beings treat each other. Trauma can also be inherited genetically. Recent work in genetics has revealed that trauma can change the expression of the DNA in our cells, and these changes can be passed from parent to child.
>
> And it gets weirder. We now have evidence that memories connected to painful events also get passed down from parent to child—and to that child's child. What's more, these experiences appear to be held, passed on, and inherited in the body, not just in the thinking brain. We are only beginning to understand how these processes work, and there are a lot of details we don't know yet. Having said that, here is what we do know so far:
>
> • A fetus growing inside the womb of a traumatized mother may inherit some of that trauma in its DNA expression. This results in the repeated release of stress hormones, which may affect the nervous system of the developing fetus.

- A man with unhealed trauma in his body may produce sperm with altered DNA expression. These, in turn, may inhibit the healthy functioning of cells in his children.

- Trauma can alter the DNA expression of a child's or grandchild's brain, causing a wide range of health and mental health issues, including memory loss, chronic anxiety, muscle weakness, and depression.

- Some of these effects seem particularly prevalent among African Americans, Jews, and American Indians, three groups who have experienced an enormous amount of historical trauma.

Some scientists theorize this genetic alteration may be a way to protect later generations. Essentially, genetic changes train our descendants' bodies through heredity rather than behavior. This suggests that what we call genetic defects may actually be ways to increase our descendants' odds of survival in a potentially dangerous environment, by relaying hormonal information to the fetus in the womb.

The womb is itself an environment: a watery world of sounds, movement, and human biochemicals. Recent research suggests that, during the last trimester of pregnancy, fetuses in the womb can learn and remember just as well as newborns. Part of what they may learn, based on what their mothers go through during pregnancy, is whether the world outside the womb is safe and healthy or dangerous and toxic. If the fetus's mother is relatively happy and healthy during her pregnancy, and if she has a nervous system that is settled, her body will produce few stress hormones.

As a result, by the time the fetus begins journeying down the birth canal, his or her body may have learned that the world is a generally safe and settled place to be. But if the fetus's mom experiences trauma, or if her earlier trauma causes a variety of stress hormones to regularly get released into her body, her baby may begin life outside the womb with less of a sense of safety, resilience, and coherence.

In Chapter 2, I share about my own family's historical trauma and how it was passed down through generations—my link to Mildred. I'm one of the lucky ones; I can connect the dots through the generations. I can trace my own trauma response back in time, which helps with the healing and with attaining greater awareness so that I can stop the cycle. But I want to shed light on and honor the wounds of the impact of historical trauma on others who are not as fortunate. I wonder about people of color, the impact of slavery, its tentacles reaching into our homes and schools, still today, and how we begin to heal a harm where individuals' histories are lost to them.

"The scars you can't see are the hardest to heal."

—ASTRID ALAUDA

"A people without the knowledge of their past history, origin and culture is like a tree without roots."

—MARCUS GARVEY

LESSONS LEARNED, INSIGHTS GAINED, AND A PROGRAM IS BORN

To honor and shine a light on this dilemma, I'd like to first share about my time as the coordinator of a Restorative Justice program in my hometown.

After my experience with Challenge Days, I realized the extent of our trauma epidemic and that we needed to build in some significant, creative, extensive supports to bring about systemic change. How do we stop the contagious effects of trauma? This is where my NVC journey really began.

In the fall of 2009, I was fortunate to participate in a nine-day Intensive NVC training in New Mexico led by Marshall Rosenberg, PhD. Marshall received his doctorate in Clinical Psychology from University of Wisconsin-Madison in 1961. However, being disillusioned with the labeling used by the field to diagnose individuals and seeking a means by which individuals could learn to be with one another in a more compassionate way, he developed Nonviolent Communication (NVC).

NVC is a system of communication used for the sole intention of connection. It has been used worldwide to address conflicts of all kinds, and Marshall's work has only grown since his passing in 2015. Chapter 3 goes into detail about the process. For now, it's important to note that after that nine-day intensive, I approached the principal of Rickards High School to see if I could teach a for-credit class in NVC. It was my eldest daughter's senior year, and I had been wondering what I could give her and her friends for graduation. What could I give them that could really show my love? After my time with Marshall, I realized that giving them NVC would be the greatest gift possible. Also, I was on a mission to find processes that could be built into schools to help reverse the trauma cycle that we see playing out in our school systems—what Challenge Days had brought to light for me. I had a hunch that NVC could serve that purpose.

I didn't realize then the gift of teaching NVC would bring to me. As with anything, if you want to learn it, teach it. This process is not something that you learn overnight or even in a semester course. It's an ongoing, evolving learning because it, ultimately, helps people reroute their thought system and their language patterns, both of which are deeply ingrained. It was a perfect setup for me to integrate the practice into my day-to-day because I was teaching it to my daughter and many of her fellow students. I often joke that if you really want to learn NVC, teach it to your daughter and then go home and live with her. I was forced to live in integrity with what I was teaching at the high school. That was more than a decade ago, and I know of several of those "teenagers" who have made NVC a cornerstone of their lives. I taught the course for two years at Rickards and also began offering workshops to adults in our community. My students at Rickards were hungry to see the program grow and, together, we approached the local Teen Center, which housed a Restorative Justice program to see if we could teach it there. I wanted to give this process to those least likely to get it and who had already suffered the consequences of conflict and ended up in our juvenile justice system.

My first-time teaching in the Restorative Justice program was disastrous. The beauty of NVC and restorative practices is that they are based on the idea that conflict typically occurs because of an imbalance of power. Restorative work is built on "power sharing" as opposed to "power over" interactions. Yet, all the youth in the program were there because they had to attend as part of their sanctions by the Florida Department of Juvenile Justice or the local State Attorney's office, or both. Mind you, I was there to teach them empathy and how to be with one another; the irony of forcing this upon them was not lost on me. So, on day 1, I tried being empathetic and giving them some choice/voice. "So, it's really important to me that you guys have some voice as we are learning. And I'm guessing most of you are pretty pissed off about being here in the first place. So, if you really don't want to be here, you can leave." Almost every kid in the circle got up and left. A few came back after a few minutes; I think they felt bad for me. I went home that night and cried to my husband. "I don't think this is going to work. How am I ever going to get cooperation and actually get them to break into dyads to learn and practice NVC empathy? The thought seemed ridiculous to me. But then, as often happens with this work, an answer came to me in the middle of the night. "What if I call on my village? I've taught this process to so many adults in my community. What if I ask enough of them to show up and then pair each youth with an adult to practice hearing and being heard deeply?" I put out the SOS and enough people showed up.

It's important to note that when teaching NVC, a big part of the process is giving people the opportunity to practice giving and receiving empathy. Empathy à la NVC is approached by providing presence, reflecting what you hear, and taking needs guesses. What we are going for with this is allowing the person who is sharing to have an experience of being deeply known and held, without any judgment. So, "Take Two" at the Restorative Justice (RJ) program. This time I circle up the youth but with an equal amount of community adults in the circle. They sit every other person—youth, adult, youth, adult, etc. When they finally get into dyads and share with one another, the outcome is rather miraculous. I literally see physical changes in the youth (facial and body expressions) in a matter of just five minutes of being heard in a different way. I've often thought it would be very interesting and revealing to see exactly what is occurring in their brains after receiving this kind of listening. I would bet there are changes that occur as a result. And that's how the instructional model of NVC came to be at the local RJ program. In fact, at the 2019 conference of the National Association of Community and Restorative Justice (NACRJ), with close to 2,000 people from across the nation in attendance, I won an award in large part for our cutting-edge program combining NVC with restorative work.

For eight years, I ran the program and continued to massage the mechanics so that we could have a place where youth could be heard so deeply that they would naturally want to cooperate and become intrinsically motivated to learn NVC, a different way of relating to themselves and others. It was a tricky undertaking. How do you get individuals mandated by a "power over" institution to be in a program, to trust the authorities in that program? We ran three fourteen-week cycles each year with about fifteen new teens and fifteen community volunteers. Our circles grew sometimes to thirty-five to forty people because we had the unusual "problem" of so many youths wanting to return as volunteers in the program and I could never turn them away. During the program cycle, youth were involved in a restorative conference on the front end where we learned how we could best serve the individual and their family. Then the youth was expected to come to the NVC class every Tuesday and Thursday for the duration of the program. This is where they learned the NVC process and how to give/receive empathy and where we modeled how to express one's needs without judgment. Also, our program staff met weekly with each program participant. It was during these individual meetings where staff and youth shared giving and receiving empathy and where, oftentimes, deep trauma was unearthed. And through the NVC process, youth would get to connect memories and current-day conflicts/challenges, seeing how many things fit together and rerouting their own and their family's trauma responses into new possibilities.

But the main reason I bring up the components of the RJ program is to help the reader understand how we built in and replicated safe connection in each cycle—connection among young/old, black/white, and individuals from various socioeconomic backgrounds. It didn't matter. And connection, we learned, is not an abstract process but a process that can be taught and replicated, and it's the key to addressing and reversing the impact of trauma. But more on this in Chapter 3. For now, I want to focus on how the NVC process is designed to help people see people and to understand each other deeply. The depth of our connection and the suffering revealed is what I want to highlight. We learned the deep stories of these teens. In fact, in Appendix A, I share some of my personal poems, with names and events changed to protect the youth. I started writing these upon waking in the morning, when these kids would weigh heavily on my mind. The poems were just a way for me to process all the secondary trauma I experienced while holding safe space for these youth. I share one of these writings here so that you can get a visceral experience of the trauma going on, often unknown.

Shaniqua

and Mo and Tray

A family torn apart
Had a home
Passed down from grandad—Shaniqua's daddy
He died—tragedy #1
But who's counting?

Hurricane Hermine
Blew the roof off
No insurance to the rescue
Mold
Rendered it uninhabitable
Family of 7 homeless
Tragedy #2
But who's counting?

New home
Joe Lewis projects
North side
For a southside family
A toxic concoction
Noted by the middle of the night
Knocks
By neighbors

Bringing guns not cake
To welcome them

And Shaniqua's daughter
Stood her ground
Her trauma response
Fight
Then arrested

The boys arrested too
They stood guard
As friends broke into local school

And Shaniqua—all what was left
Sat in her broken home
Surrounded by filth
Her depression couldn't clean
As she pieced together a plan to keep her project home
The eviction notice came
Due to the arrests—the fight
No place for south side on north side
No ear to hear the reasons
Is this tragedy #4 or 5?
Losing count

The boys—
Mo quiet with a grudge towards mom.
Tray—superstar smile. Roll with the punches.
Bedroom was a living room couch.

They loved their mama's mac and cheese.
Loved their mama's cooking

They shared that with me
After she was found dead
Out of nowhere
Wondering if it was natural
Or done to her?
Tragedy 6?

Moved in with grandma
Couldn't keep track of the number in that house
Grandma—seemed to care
Or was it the monthly check that came along with the crew
Helping to feed her addiction

We dropped off food
Got the boys summer jobs
All we could think of to do

Within a year
Grandma dead too
Mo became a daddy
Fought with his love
Now doing time

I see Tray at school
Still smiling
No one knows

Tragedies he's been through
We lost count long ago

Shrugged our shoulders out of sorrow and despair
Not lack of care
Much easier to turn away
Then to stare at it all up close
And wonder where to start
Where to start—the repair.

Ashamed to say
I'm out of here
Running back to my safe white world
With my first-world problems

And Shaniqua
Rolls over in her grave
For the family she couldn't save.

DECONTEXTUALIZED TRAUMA

After deeply listening to people for so many years, I am amazed by the amount of trauma most of our African American youth are walking around with. And the trauma is handed down genetically and retriggered by those around them. I would say that even those of us who consider ourselves professionals have a long way to go to understand the depth of trauma in our schools and systems and the way that our own thoughts, interactions, and communications can oftentimes retrigger a trauma response. This is further exacerbated because most individuals do not contextualize historical trauma as such. We see a youth "misbehaving" or "acting out" and label it and react to it without a full understanding of the historical trauma in play at that moment. Usually, the youth and his family are, also, unaware of the connection to how the youth is showing up and how past events have influenced how the child thinks and reacts in any given circumstance. It's all quite complex and complicated further because most people have yet to develop communication skills to help slow all of this down, and unearth the needs that are in play.

This is why the Nonviolent Communication process has real potential in helping to create a new world, a world where trauma begins to be healed and ceases to be handed down from one generation to the next. Chapter 3 goes into detail about the Nonviolent Communication process and the multiple ways in which it can be key in interrupting the trauma cycle that tends to play out in society like a domino effect—one person's trauma response triggering another person's trauma response and so on through the ages. We see this dysfunction everywhere without realizing it's not dysfunction at all but unhealed trauma. In fact, most of the disconnection we see in all parts of society, in our politics, schools, communities —the violence everywhere that seems to be escalating with no easy solution—all of it is rooted in historical trauma working in its unconscious ways.

This book was written to highlight the magic of NVC and its potential to stop the dominoes from falling. It was inspired by my mother's death, our own history of trauma, and the gift that NVC has been in healing it. In the next chapter, I want to share about my family's historical trauma. Then I will go into extensive detail about NVC, what it is, and why I believe it has tremendous potential to advance our societies.

CHAPTER 2

OUR STORY

*"If you look deeply into the palm of your hand, you
will see your parents and all generations of your ancestors.
All of them are alive in this moment.
Each is present in your body. You are the
continuation of these people."*

—THICH NHAT HANH

My relationship with my mother was complicated. My mother was complicated. Passionate to an extreme, even right to the end. She had the perfect death—more on that later. This passion was on both ends of the continuum: extreme love, fun, compassion, care and extreme judgment, conflict, anger, and disconnection. The dedication at the beginning of this book, "Our Lesson on Love," was inspired by a song that I was given the morning after we learned that there was no treatment for her cancer. Mind you, her illness seemed to come out of nowhere. Yes, the lung cancer that killed her must have been there for a bit, but I wonder about the timing of all of this and its connection to our history. And if there is more to all of this than what medical science can explain?

In recent months, the world has been sickened by the events in Eastern Europe where Putin's Russian troops have been invading Ukraine and Americans have been suddenly bombarded with nightly news images of everyday people, looking like you and me, amid carnage. To be honest, I haven't seen any of it because I gave up news about a year ago and seem to get what I need just by everyday conversation. But, my mother, she watched it every day until she, too, in the past month shut it off. She shared how watching those images did something to her very deeply, how they unearthed something hidden within. It was like her ancestors came alive in her and my five-foot mama's cells remembered and woke with the trauma from the same place in the world but, roughly, one hundred years earlier. Doctors say lung cancer killed her, but I wonder if it was Ukraine that did?

GREAT GRANDMA MILDRED

Mildred was my mother's grandmother on her father's side. She died when I was quite young, but I do remember visiting her at the "old age home" and not enjoying it much. The smell, the sight of old people wasting away, it wasn't fun. But my mom would take us to visit Grandma Mildred; she was my mother's hero. I've heard the story of Grandma Mildred many times throughout my life. Here's the short version.

In the late 1800s into the early twentieth century, Jews were being persecuted and exiled from Russia-Poland, the same area of the world of the Russian/Ukraine war. For those who know, think *Fiddler on the Roof.* I think of *Fiddler on the Roof* as my family's story. If you haven't watched the movie, I highly recommend it. Grandma Mildred and her mother, father, and siblings were forced to leave their home in Russia-Poland, get out or die, because of their Jewish heritage. Please slow down on that last sentence. Don't wash over it too fast. Take it in! Imagine, for a moment, the utter fear and disruption to a person's emotional and physical state to be unearthed from one's home, the place of security and knowing, and step into a future where one's basics of food, water, and shelter were all unknown. They were exiting with guns at their backs—leaving for fear of their lives because they practiced a particular faith and way of life. Those images on the nightly news of Ukraine were, for my mother, a portal back to her grandmother's experience.

According to our family lore, Grandma Mildred was eleven or twelve when her family was forced to leave her homeland. Her family fled to England for refuge. However, Mildred decided she wanted to go to America. She had a boyfriend in New York City, and with letter in hand from this boy, she boarded a ship to the United States to reunite with this young man, leaving her family and European life behind.

She spent roughly five days in the bottom of the ship, in the steerage class. The journey of steerage is nearly universally described as miserable. Passengers experienced overcrowding, foul air, filth, intense seasickness, and inedible food. She was one of the strong ones to exit at Ellis Island, where the ships would sail past the Statue of Liberty and then unload their passengers. These immigrants were processed and allowed to step foot into this new and strange world.

Of course, Mildred never found her boyfriend. New York and America were much larger than her eleven-year-old brain could fathom. Not speaking a word of English, she was greeted by other Jewish immigrants when she unloaded from the ship and was "processed" at Ellis Island. These other immigrants showed her the ropes and got her housing and a job sewing at the sweat factories. She married young, at age fifteen, and had three children: Morris, Ben, and Rose. Ben was my grandfather, my mother's father.

Back then, before labor laws were passed, people in the factories were expected to work brutal hours. Work or starve, that was the choice. Grandma Mildred's husband contracted tuberculosis and was sent out west for the dry air. Mildred worked and raised her children as best she could, though hours at the job kept her from being there with her offspring. In fact, her first-born, Morris, died at home alone at age thirteen. Mildred had to leave him to go to work while he stayed home with meningitis. Her other two children, Ben (my Poppy) and Rose (my Aunt Rose), were sent to an orphanage because my grandmother wasn't around enough to care for them. Again, another famous movie, *Oliver Twist*, comes to mind. Turn-of-the-century orphanages were not the kindest of places. My grandfather would run away often because he hated it there, but when he did, his sister would be beaten, and he would be beaten when they found him.

NANA AND POPPY

This is the story of my grandfather's trauma, handed to him innocently, due to the circumstances of *his* mother's life. It gets even better. When his own father passed, Mildred went to the Social Security office to set up payments, only to find out that her husband and father of her children had a whole other family who had already come to claim his Social Security. Poppy learned, at around age sixteen, that he was a "bastard," which in those days was akin to a curse. And for this he cursed and disconnected from his mother, their relationship badly bruised forever. It's no wonder he had rage. He came by it innocently. It was handed to him.

And that rage, all that pent-up disappointment, all that pent-up anger and childhood fear, where could it possibly go? It had to go somewhere! Fast forward, he falls in love with Rhoda, my grandmother; we called her Nana. Here is a picture of them at Coney Island (Figure 4).

Figure 4: Nana and Poppy at Coney Island.

I love this picture; it captures a moment in history. The bathing suits. My Nana, who always seemed rather conservative to me, on Ben's shoulders. How cool is that? He really loved her. But they didn't know what they were doing. They had no template on how to be parents, how to have a family. And what they did have…was trauma. Survive—fight, flight, freeze. Even Nana's family had its own horror. She would tell me about her mother, Ann, how she was the kindest person in the world and how she died of a sudden heart attack after answering the door and receiving the telegram that her entire family—mother, father, sisters, and brothers—were all wiped out, shot, and killed by the Nazis. My Nana's mother, Ann, died with that telegram in her hand.

MARCIA AND ANN

What happens to people when trauma occurs and is never realized or processed? It lives on. It comes out in other ways and at other times when fear and extreme emotions emerge. So now Ben and Rhoda have their own two children, my beloved mother Marcia and Ann (later called Marci and Toni.) My mother had reflux as a baby. This is another one of those lines that the reader should take in slowly. It's just a sentence but it carries a lot of weight. My mother could not keep down food as a baby; she would projectile vomit everything she ate. Imagine how scary, gross, and exhausting that was for Rhoda and Ben, who were also working crazy hours to get by—he as a cab driver and she at the local fruit market. No one taught them how to parent; no one taught them how to talk to their children or even themselves when things were hard and emotions were high. Instead, my grandparents fed my mother her vomit as a baby. They were frustrated, overwhelmed, uneducated. They thought she was vomiting on purpose. The abuse did not stop there. Ben's anger would erupt often, especially when Rhoda was upset with the children. My mom was beaten (not just hit) on the regular. At five, since her parents worked long hours, my mother was left alone a lot; she oversaw the cooking and cleaning and, eventually, the care of her sister, Toni.

The dysfunction caused by unprocessed, historical trauma carried over into that relationship too. On my mother's dying bed, she was ashamed, but asked that her sister not attend her funeral. A lifetime of hurt was never healed. Perhaps it will be in her next lifetime? As young children, they were unknowingly pit against one another. Mom took care of Toni. Toni had a learning disability (undiagnosed dyslexia); things didn't come easy for Toni. Mom was the "perfect" one. Toni got Mom's hand-me-downs since they were poor. Mom would sometimes get beat when Toni made too much noise when my mom was watching her as their parents slept. They were set up; it was a perfect recipe for jealousy, competition, and resentment to grow. And grow it did. Early on, though, Mom looked out for T, trying to protect her from their father's wrath. After my mother was married to my father, Toni, age seventeen, visited them with bruises all over her face. My mother went to the courts and got custody of Toni. Mom had to face her parents in court and, she told me, it was years before her father would speak with her again. She told me this story, once again, on her dying bed, trying to get me to understand how she had been there for her sister and how her sister had done things that deeply hurt her over the years. Her own trauma did not allow awareness or trust to be rebuilt, even though Toni had reached out several times, trying to mend what was broken. The relationship with her sister and their childhood history, in general, brought up deep, unconscious, confusing fear and consequential resentment for my mother.

MY MOM—THE FIGHTER

There is more, much more, but let's just say my mom suffered her own trauma. And those of us with trauma tend to operate in survival mode. We fight, freeze up, or run away at the least sign of real or perceived threat. My mother... she was a fighter. She came by it honestly, just like her own father.

As mentioned in the chapter on trauma, people who experience it repeatedly in childhood tend to be on heightened alert for threat in their environment. The amygdala has a knee-jerk reaction whenever there is a real or a perceived threat to the person. Two main ways my mother would "fight" were with her voice tone and volume level, and with her words and judgements. It's easy for me to see why she adopted these survival tactics. Imagine being beaten throughout the years, starting from a very young age, small, powerless. Physically, her protection was her voice. Plus, her father used a similar technique of yelling and using judgments; she copied what she saw modeled. She was an itty, bitty thing, all of five feet at her peak, but, man, you did not want to cross her or set her off.

Mom carried with her all the intensity that her father had unknowingly passed down to her, but she never beat us. That level of abuse stopped with her, thankfully. I read once that "each generation improves upon the last," and I can see this truth in my own lineage. My mother yelled when upset. She screamed and pointed her finger. Very occasionally, she would throw things. Once, I saw her hit my brother in a way that I would say was bordering on abusive. The rest of her hard physical contact was more in line with a parent spanking her child, but these were not beatings. However, when her fight response did occur, I often wouldn't see the rage coming. Life was a mixture of many wonderful moments, but they could quickly turn sour and scary. In fairness, the wonderful moments were, likely, more plentiful than the difficult ones, but they both left an impact. And as we learned in Chapter 1, the hippocampus tends to hold onto negative memories and bury the more positive ones.

To better understand the impact of my mother's "fight" response on me, it's important to talk a bit about brain research and how our brains work. In particular, let's discuss the default mode network (DMN). Here is an excerpt from Sarah Peyton's book, *Your Resonant Self*, that explains the importance of the DMN and its impact on how we move and think in the world.

The Default Mode Network is active when we are not paying attention to the external world. Our brain automatically brings together memory and thought and integrates both with our sense of self. Research shows that the DMN is universal in all humans and that it starts immediately as soon as we stop focusing on externals, in as little time as one second between algebra problems and the tiny brains of two-day-old infants.

The Default Mode Network (DMN). What does your inner voice sound like? The one that is inside your head that only you can hear? If you stop for a moment to notice what it feels like to be you, you will find that you have a particular attitude about yourself... Often the inner voice can seem devoid of emotion altogether, but whatever its tone, it tends to flow in an endless stream of chatter about the good, the bad, and the ugly: who we are, what we've done, what we've forgotten, and what the other people in our lives have done, haven't done, or are going to do... The pattern that runs automatically in our heads, when our brain is not engaged in doing something intentional, is our inner voice. Even if we can't hear this voice, we might guess what its tone is from the way we treat ourselves or from the way we are thinking about others. If we have had experiences of being known and delighted in by people who have been important to us (such as parents, grandparents, teachers, or even a kind neighbor), our thoughts may have an easy, gentle tone.

If people have had other life experiences—such as having parents or spouses who want to improve them and only speak to them to make them "better," who are exhausted and want their children or partners to be seen and not heard, or who are surrounded by too much busyness or are too overwhelmed to see them at all—then a person's inner voice may sound very different. For many people, this inner voice can be unrelentingly negative and sometimes even vicious.

HOW MY DEFAULT MODE NETWORK WAS FORMED

In this section, I provide some background on how my mother interacted with me and others (because of her own trauma and DMN), how some of the significant events of my life occurred because of the fallout of these interactions, and how all of this is in play in my default mode network.

As indicated previously, my mother, when upset, screamed relentlessly, pointed her finger in my face, told me I was selfish and inconsiderate. My mother would scream in this way, and often I wouldn't see it coming. One minute the world would be well, and the next minute all hell would break loose. I have a memory of her tirades and how they would come in phases. First you would receive the initial onslaught of intensity, words, and judgments. Then she would leave, and I would sigh with relief, thinking it's over, only for her to return and continue the assault. This coming and going would occur several times, creating a strong sense of anxiety, never knowing when the coast was clear.

And this fight response of hers would surface in her intimate relationships, with her children and her spouses. My first memory of it was during a family trip to New York City. My father was driving, and my brother, sister, and I were in the back seat. We stopped for gas, and when getting back in the car, my father accidentally closed the door on Mom's hand. Of course, anyone would respond angrily in a moment like that, so some grace is extended to my mother. But the intensity, the meanness of what she said to him, and the persistence of what I would call verbal abuse was out of alignment even with getting one's hand stuck in a door. I remember my father looking scared, deflated, so sad and embarrassed, and I remember feeling shocked and very scared. I was probably about six at the time.

Yet, again, another trip to New York City highlights the inconsistency in my experiences with my mother. They were either filled with love and delight or fear and horror. I remember taking a trip into the city one time in her green El Dorado Cadillac convertible. On the way home, she had the top down, but it was a bit cool out, so she turned the heat on. I loved that for some reason. It was a beautiful day, and we'd had a great time in the city. So, with the top down, heat blasting, music playing, my mother, just to be silly and shocking and to make me laugh, started flashing her boobs as we were driving. And we laughed and joked the whole way home. I was around eleven at the time.

These two trips to New York capture the complexity of my relationship with my mother. She was my biggest fan. She would often tell me, "You're going to be famous one day." She would console me when life was hard. She tickled my head and did this great thing of putting her finger, with her long-manicured nails, in my ear as my head would lie in her lap. I loved that so much. But, when she was upset, holy shit. I learned to be very quiet during her tirades. *Just be quiet and this will be over faster.* My trauma response was not fight, it was to flee or freeze. But before I go deeper into my own trauma response, I'd like to share a bit more about the trickle-down impact of Mom's trauma and her survival practices.

As I share here, I have concerns that the reader will hear blame toward my mother. This morning I looked up the definition of blame which is "to assign responsibility for a fault or wrong." This is the last thing I want in writing this book; in fact, my intention is the opposite. I am completely aware that my mother's personality was shaped, largely, by events years before she was born, just like all of us. As mentioned earlier, there is even scientific brain-based research now that shows how trauma response is passed down genetically. The blame game that we tend to play is, in large part, the passive cause of what keeps our internal and external violence going. It's the underlying cause of the epidemic trauma I am trying desperately to reverse. In Chapters 3 and 4, I discuss, at length, the practice of Nonviolent Communication (NVC) developed by Marshall Rosenberg, PhD, and my business, The Bigbie Method, which was created to help scale NVC to all areas of society. My mother was the biggest believer in my work, and she understood its intimate link to the life we experienced together. We often talked, in awe, of the blessing and irony of how our life story has morphed into a body of work with the potential to bring about world peace. Truly, if I can get my point across here—and people everywhere learn and apply NVC—that is what is possible. Mom asked me to write this story to help others understand the unconscious forces alive in our interactions, how to bring them to light, and reroute our brains' ingrained responses. In NVC, we learn how to recognize when we are in blame mode and use a completely different way of communicating what we need rather than making someone wrong for their actions. So, reader, as you go forth and read about what may be perceived as my mother's faults, please note they are not told in that light.

My mother was a deeply spiritual being. She had a depth to her and a deep love of the mystery of life and beyond. She passed that to me even with all the "crazy" that happened in our life. Also, some may wonder, what about my father? Why am I only talking about the impact of my mother's family? To be honest, my father was always a figure in the background. When my parents divorced, he and I were estranged for thirty-seven years, but with no bitterness. Yet, even before that point, my mother was my world; she shaped my world. She was always the greatest force in my life, in all our lives. Everyone else seemed to pale in comparison to this tiny, five-foot, barely one-hundred-pound woman.

MOM'S MARRIAGES

Mom was married and divorced three times. Each of these relationships had its own complexity and good cause for my mother to want out. Each of her husbands had his own dysfunction to add to the mix. My father didn't have enough depth to keep her interest. He worked a lot to build their small empire and was not physically or emotionally available, and then there was the addiction issue. They came into wealth after living with little, and drugs, high society, and a fast life took their toll. Her second husband, who I saw most as a father, eventually revealed a sexual addiction, and she learned he had, for years, been engaging with prostitutes weekly. And her third husband, who had witnessed the violent killing of many of his family members in a home robbery as a teenager, was known to react to Mom with rage when his frustration and need for emotional safety and being heard were unmet. While he appeared to be an easy-going, kind-hearted soul, I believe he hit her at least once and, occasionally, referred to her as a "fucking bitch" to her face and used other obscenities when upset. Note, each of her husbands used his own trauma response to come back to a sense of wholeness and safety. My dad would run away and freeze his emotions with drugs and alcohol. Her second husband used sex. And her third husband would freeze and then explode into fight. The last marriage brought up a huge need for physical and emotional safety, similar to what Mom experienced as a child. She needed to get out of each of these marriages.

Rarely is the breakdown of a relationship one-sided, however. My mother was a complicated package of extremes. As indicated earlier, she was filled with love, fun, and joy, but her anger could appear almost out of nowhere, and things could turn sour quickly. When upset, she had the trauma response of literally and metaphorically pointing her finger at the other. In NVC terms, she jackaled out quite a bit, meaning she was quick to blame the other person and point out his faults to his face and to others when he was not around. This happened even before the drugs started with my dad, the sex with my stepdad, and the escalated verbal arguments with her third husband. Never did I hear her reflect on her part in those breakups, and each one was brutal—lots of arguments, insults, and all three divorces resulted in bitterness and disconnection.

JUDGING OTHERS

Looking through the frame of her own upbringing, it makes sense that she learned this habit of yelling and making judgmental statements of the other. As a child, othering the other was how she could make sense of the abuse coming toward her. It also makes sense that she talked about people to other people. She needed protection. Protection from her childhood trauma that was never heard or processed at the time, trauma that lived on. So, people who did "bad" things to her were "bad" people from whom she needed protection. Her whole life she sought the protection of a parent that she never received as a child. She tried to get this as an adult by angrily talking about the people with whom she was in conflict to other people in her life who loved her.

As a child, she would tell me things about my father that no child should hear. Some of it was observational, like her retelling things he shared about sleeping with other women in the downstairs bedroom of our house when they were separated. But much of what she shared was her judgmental interpretations of his wrongness or badness. "He's disgusting, demented, stupid, selfish. He thinks only of himself." She was hurting and scared in these situations. And, again, in the context of her own childhood abuse, it stands to reason that she would want friends and family to be on her side. It was her way of saying, "Please see him as bad. Please help protect me. Please verify that I'm not bad or have done something wrong to deserve this."

If she had said those things with fear and humility, instead of with anger and judgment, we may have been able to hear her pain and fear. But what I never could do was hate the others or completely, emotionally disconnect myself from them the way she wanted me to. It was almost like she needed the people in her life to hate and disconnect from the person with whom she was in conflict so she could have safety. I was not wired to do that, especially when none of her husbands had ever treated us (me, my brother, or sister) badly. In fact, we had the opposite experience every time. All three spouses met needs of kindness, care, and support of us, her children. It's hard to disconnect from someone when you have a direct experience of kindness and when the person saying "mean" things about them has done the same to you. Plus, paradoxically, my mother had modeled extreme love and compassion to us and others when she was not operating in her fear reflex. I think this shaped my ability to see the full picture.

All this disconnection was no one's fault, and disconnecting further would only perpetuate the sickness in which we swam. I didn't want to create hate, make hate where I didn't experience hate, just to prove my love to her. Thankfully, in the end, I believe our story, her story, ended with me showing and her finally experiencing the love she so badly needed to know *without* perpetuating hate toward others. This is why I wrote the final chapter of this book—to share how healing can actually occur; how love can triumph. For now, back to my DMN.

THE FALLOUT

To understand more about my DMN, it's important that you know the impact on my family of our parents' divorce. When my parents split, we lived in a mansion of the time. With no formal education and my mother's support, my father built a huge collection agency business. They moved from their tiny Bronx apartment to, eventually, our three-story Redwood home, complete with an indoor swimming pool, sauna, exercise room, two kitchens, and a bar. We had a laundry chute and an intercom system throughout the house. My brother, sister, and I each had our own bedrooms, phone lines, and dogs. Pierre was hired to take care of the house, cook, chauffeur us kids, and occasionally massage my father.

In what seemed like a blink of an eye, we went from that to the complete opposite. Owing to the disconnection and bitterness between my parents and my father going AWOL (thanks to drugs and literally running from the Mafia because of some poor business decisions), our life changed overnight. My mother, who didn't work, was forced into action and figure out how to pay the bills and take care of her children. On top of everyday bills, she was being pursued by debt collectors because of a huge loan she had co-signed for my father's business. Long story short, we moved from New York to Miami Beach, Florida, but told everyone we knew that we were moving to California—to dodge the bill collectors. We lost every relative, every friend—the whole world we ever knew was gone, even our dogs were left behind. I was fourteen at the time, in ninth grade, a freshman in high school.

We moved from that huge house in New York and settled into a two-bedroom, cockroach-infested apartment in Miami Beach where my brother, sister, and I shared a room with mattresses on the floor. But it wasn't losing the material things that hurt, honestly. It was losing all the connections we had ever known. I was forbidden to talk to any of my friends from New York because my mother didn't want the debt collectors to find us. To make matters worse, I ended up in two middle schools and three high schools in three years, and I had the humiliating experience of going from middle school to high school back to middle school. How was that possible? In New York, I attended eighth grade at Clarkstown Middle School and half of ninth grade at Clarkstown High School North. Then when we moved to Florida, in the middle of my ninth-grade year, I went back to middle school, Nautilus Middle School, and the next year attended tenth grade at Miami Beach High School. Then, my mother sold the New York house and bought a modest home in Hollywood, Florida, and we moved again, and I attended eleventh through twelfth grades at South Broward High School.

During this time, my mother was under enormous stress, trying to figure out how to feed her family. She was absent quite a lot, and when she was around, during the Miami Beach years, the stress would explode toward us often. Teenage years can be difficult all on their own. But the combination of literally losing our world, having to re-establish my social life in five different schools, and my mother being unpredictably angry and explosive made my teenage years even more interesting than usual. Couple all of that with being shy-natured, I struggled socially and academically.

I would like to share a few key memories of my teen years here, for the sake of bringing about greater clarity on the psychological impact of trauma. I want people to understand my story and pit it side-by-side with that picture of Challenge Days that I shared earlier—the vastness of our trauma problem. I want readers to see my pains in the context of the local RJ program and all the deep trauma I had the privilege and devastation of hearing. I know one person's trauma cannot/should not be compared to another. But I'm hoping to explain how my trauma (which in my mind seems to pale in comparison to so many of the stories I have been entrusted to hear) showed up in those formative years and then how it has impacted me as an adult, an adult who has done a lot of conscious work, unlike many others, around mitigating it. I want people to get the breadth and complexity of the trauma issue and its impact on our children, our schools, our society. I also want you to know that I have a solution for turning the epidemic of trauma around. I will not leave you hanging. For now, let me continue about my journey in high school.

Besides the tough interactions I experienced with my mom over the years, I had other events that left their harsh mark on my DMN and my brain's trauma response, which is to run away or freeze in the face of danger. I do not blame my mother for these experiences. However, if we did not have the dysfunction in our family, and hers in her family of origin, and so on, these events would never have occurred, and the way I unconsciously learned to speak to myself would have been different. Again, I think about all the kids in the world and the current and historical events shaping their inner voice. Here are some of mine.

- ▶ We moved from New York in January 1979. I remember my first day at Nautilus Middle School, where I officially went from high school back to middle school in ninth grade. I enrolled in the school right at lunchtime, and I remember walking into this huge, loud cafeteria, wondering where I would sit. I knew no one. Feeling so insecure, against the rules (and I was not a rule breaker), I walked out of the cafeteria and wandered the halls, crying.

- Since I was seven years of age, I had the greatest blessing of attending two months of summer camp in New York at Camp Kinderring. It was my happy place. Once we moved to Florida and lost all our money, my time at KR came to a halt. Between ninth and tenth grades, I could not return because we couldn't afford it. Instead, I attended the Miami Beach Jewish Community Center as Counselor in Training, and I met one of my first friends. Joji lived up the street from my roach-infested apartment, but in a different world. In Miami Beach, there are pockets of wealthy neighborhoods. She lived in one of them. We spent most days of that entire summer together at her house. But when school started and we both began Miami Beach High, she didn't talk or look at me. Beach High was a difficult place for me, trying to gain self-esteem. The school had sororities and, if you weren't in one, you were treated like you were nobody. I remember sitting in the auditorium for driver's ed in my assigned seat with the sorority girls surrounding me. They talked to one another as if I wasn't even there—completely invisible. I remember sitting in my English class, not saying a word, feeling very depressed and insecure. I had lost all my confidence, even in a subject area in which I once had a lot of pride. I failed

Algebra that year, the first time I had ever failed anything in school. I remember being in social situations where I couldn't find my thoughts and was stifled while speaking. I was told years later by a therapist that this was literally my brain in freeze mode, trying to make sense of the best way to protect my sense of self.

▶ I did make a few friends, some people on the fringes of high school society. And I had the run of Miami Beach because the K bus stopped right outside our apartment and my mother wasn't around to monitor my coming and going. I also got my first real job, working at a Barton's Candy Story at the beach. That helped me retain some dignity and helped me save up money so that I could return to Camp Kinderring the following summer, which was my last year as a camper. I returned several years thereafter in a working capacity.

▶ I bring up Kinderring here because several years prior to the writing of this book, a brain research therapist asked me why (after all the things that happened to me growing up) was I relatively stable—why was I able to function successfully in day-to-day events and stressors? My trauma didn't seem to fully stifle me; in fact, in ways, it informed me. I theorize it was a mixture of the intense love and support that my mother provided throughout the years (when it wasn't all the other stuff) and my time at Camp Kinderring. I think KR saved me. There, I was revered. I wasn't invisible. I was a star. People loved and saw me deeply. Everyone was a friend, and many were admirers. I would repeatedly receive the greatest honors for my character. I won torchbearer in the summer between eleventh and twelfth grades. It's a hard thing to explain to outsiders, but to people who know Camp Kinderring, it's a big deal. Figure 5 is a picture of me lighting the torch. To this day, several decades later, I get invited back each summer to help pass the torch to future generations.

► When I came back from camp after the summer of my tenth grade, we moved to Hollywood, Florida, and I enrolled in South Broward High School. I fell in love for the first time that summer, at camp, with a boy who was super smart and who had great academic ambitions. He had a large influence on me, and I made the conscious decision that year to focus solely on academics to bring up my suffering GPA. Also, I was tired of trying to make friends and be a part of a high school social community, considering that this was my fifth school in three years. So, for my entire eleventh-grade year, I spoke to not one person my age. That's no lie. I knew no one and had not one friend or acquaintance. I remember eating outside the library every day at lunch by myself, book in hand, pretending to read so that I could cover the shame I felt about being alone and friendless.

Figure 5: Kinderring Torchbearer

Most of these events were never known by others. I had no adult to hear and to help me make sense of all the struggles. No one knew the deep inadequacy and shame I experienced sitting in tenth-grade English or sitting outside that library while in eleventh grade. No one was there to help me make sense of that or to help me integrate and timestamp my mother's rage when it occurred. Without such resonance, a deep knowing, it's near impossible for one's brain to let go of and store these experiences in their proper place where they won't taint one's future perceptions.

After sporadic therapy and years of spiritual work, I can see the workings of the divine in all these experiences. I can also see how my mother's passed-down trauma response and how the fallout of those reactions shape the way I move in the world as an adult. As a youth, I remember walking into the entranceway on the side of my house, often with a pit in my stomach, wondering, *Is today going to be a good day or a bad day? Am I in trouble for something?*

MY LINK TO MILDRED

Now, as an adult, I still look for signs of being in trouble. Is someone angry or upset with me? This is especially painful if I don't see it coming, if I don't understand the upset. It will literally spiral me into protection mode. I experience fear and internal tension, my mind goes to lots of rationalizing, trying to figure out them and the situation, trying to save my sense of self or okayness. This happens, also, when I hear people speaking judgmentally about others or if there is limited communication where a story of judgment can arise. I feel fear. I notice in new situations that I experience a subtle unease until I have a sense of connection with the new people, until I know we can be with one another in an emotionally safe way—where everyone is extended love and grace. To be clear, you would never know this. I move through the world with a lot of external success; I power through my internal experience, but the stress is often present.

I also get scared and nervous when I'm with people in power, people who have more power than I do, to make decisions. Most of our organizational structures in business, schools, and government are hierarchical; thus, the power-over structure is built in. I've found I work best outside of such structures. I think that most of our systems are not set up to ensure people are heard and to experience that their voice matters, and this, coupled with my childhood experiences, is very painful. This is all, in a sense, my link to Mildred. It is also what drives the work I do in the world; that's where divinity comes into play.

So, back to the default mode network, and let's tie all this together with my own DMN. First, remember in the previous chapter, I shared some core ideas. These ideas are also connected to the main principles of Cognitive Behavior Therapy: (1) our beliefs are informed by our childhood experiences, and (2) humans tend to hold onto the negative more easily than the positive, and this shows up as automatic negative thoughts. It's only since I started writing this book that I am catching the way my DMN plays out for me. I've always thought I had a pretty "good" inner voice, an inner voice that met needs for self-love and self-esteem, but I've recently noticed that it's not that way consistently, just like my childhood interactions with my mother. I have an inner voice that nurtures, loves, and uplifts, but there is also this critical voice hiding inside and, coming into awareness of it, I am amazed that its messages mirror the critical messages said to and experienced by me as a child. I'm also beginning to understand how it takes away from my God-given self-love and for my love of others. There is something very practical and spiritual about my journey of trauma, pain, and love that I pray I can convey adequately in words and in a way that is helpful to others.

Remember in Chapter 1, we discussed the amygdala and how it is constantly asking, "Am I safe? Do I matter?" As Sarah Peyton explains in *Your Resonant Self*:

Major injuries to body and heart are not the only kinds of trauma. Anything that has happened in the past that hurts us now is trauma, and we are the only ones who get to say whether something is traumatic. Nobody else can tell you that your pain isn't real... Your pain is valid and true, and if someone had been there to share it with you, it would not hurt as much as it does now. Neural networks that hold pain persist because we didn't get any support to help us connect them back up to the rest of our brain and make sense of them. We didn't receive empathy [as defined and explained in Chapter 3]. This support can be as simple as the welcome and acknowledgement provided by warm community.

Some people may not see my experiences as traumatic, but it fits that definition. There is a definite connection between what happens after a traumatic event or circumstance, how much we are held and heard, the level of connection we receive that helps us better connect to self and make sense of the event and, therefore, put it in its proper place in our memory. The degree of connection and processing of the trauma is indicative of the burden we will likely carry in the years following the traumatic event/circumstance. It is critical that the person experiencing the trauma has a sense that someone notices, someone cares, someone believes them. Void of that kind of connection or resonance, the trauma will live on often in unconscious and disruptive ways. The trauma is underlying the default mode network and the ways we learn to talk to ourselves about ourselves and the world around us.

Since my mother's passing, I have been struggling with three specific things, and I am able to see the way my past trauma is playing out in my interactions, with the underlying culprit being the way that I talk to myself—my DMN.

First, the fact that I feel at peace about my mother's passing. When I started writing this book, I was able to embrace it. But now, as time goes on, I notice an unsteadiness, a critical voice, a bodily tension, and an uncertainty about my reaction to her death. I am doubting myself and my reaction. *Is it okay? Am I okay? How can I be okay? Is there something wrong with me? Am I insensitive, selfish—just living my life with happiness in her void?* Notice the script and how similar it is to the script my mother would yell at me? This is my link to Mildred.

The second thing that's been hard around her death is that I have a very close friend who did not speak with me during the month of her illness or since her death, even after I reached out to her several times. This friend also knew and cared for my mother. I, honestly, have no idea why she has been absent; it's baffling. But I've had some great insights into how my DMN operates in these circumstances. First, I felt angry and deeply hurt and, in all honesty, I still go there but to a lesser degree. The hurt and anger come because of my DMN. My mind searches for what I did wrong. *Why is she so angry with me that she hasn't talked with me during such a hard time? I'm in trouble; I did something wrong; someone is mad at me, and I don't know why.* Sound familiar? The old script, the "crazy" handed down to me, my link to Mildred. And the DMN doesn't end with self-doubt; it goes into blame of others to protect myself from the unconscious voice wreaking havoc on my inner being. *What the heck is wrong with her? She always does this shutting-down thing. I thought she was supposed to be a friend.* When I can sit back and look at the whole situation through the lens of the Nonviolent Communication (NVC) process, I am able to reroute the critical voice back to some love of self and other. More about NVC to come. For now, I want the reader to understand the connection between my mother's history and my DMN and how it shows up in my interactions if I remain unaware and unable to reroute it.

The last challenge, since Mom died, has been some of the interactions with my sister, Lynda, my best friend in life. I love her so much. She has been suffering tremendously since our mother's death and was avoiding talking to me because she said she was having too rough of a time and that something happened during Mom's Celebration of Life that was super painful for her. My DMN: *I did something wrong! Someone is mad at me. I'm in trouble and I don't even know what I did. Maybe she is mad because I'm not in pain over Mom's death. She's so much more caring than me. I'm so inconsiderate. What's wrong with me? Mom died and I don't even care.* I notice the pattern of these inner conversations (similar to the words my mother would yell at me) along with anger toward my sister—my inner voice mobilizing into judgment of her, protecting my own sense of self by making her "wrong." My link to Mildred, my own trauma trigger—until I can stop, notice what I'm doing, notice my inner voice, and hold both of us with compassion for the needs in play. That is NVC in action.

More to come on that, but for now, I want to point out there is extreme truth in the idea that you must first love yourself to love others. I am understanding that concept more deeply because of these latest challenges.

My link to Mildred shows up in other ways as well. As mentioned earlier, I notice something in me that is nervous whenever I am in social situations where people use judgmental language, or if I don't know anyone well. I notice tension and fear internally in work situations where there is no shared power and the person in charge isn't open to hearing me or others. All these situations have the imprint of my developmental years and the way my mother interacted with me because of how her parents interacted with her, and so on and so on. And, as indicated in Chapter 1, not only am I impacted by the external fight, flight, freeze response, but passed-down genetic coding is also in play.

Even with all of that, there is good news. You can hear, understand, and transform your inner voice if you don't enjoy the way it treats you. Also, there is a way that we can learn to talk with one another that is designed to keep all parties emotionally safe *and* heard deeply. In the two years before my mother passed, she started listening to my podcast on NVC, *It's All About Connection*, and began rerouting her communication/thinking processes. We had some very connecting and healing conversations, with the final one being just months before she unexpectedly died.

In the next chapter, I want to share more deeply about Nonviolent Communication and how it has the potential to break the cycle and epidemic of trauma. I know it works because I'm living it.

In the last chapter of this book, I will share the intimate details of my mother's final month with us and the miracle and never-ending evolution of love and healing work.

CHAPTER 3

NONVIOLENT COMMUNICATION

Breaking the Cycle of Trauma

*"Connection is the experience of ease and flow
that occurs within and between peoplewhen they are
seen, heard, and valued without judgment."*

In Chapter 1, we went into detail about trauma and established that
we have a trauma epidemic on hand. Roughly two-thirds of us had
some traumatic event and/or circumstance between the ages of zero
and seventeen, and our brains are wired to be on heightened alert
regarding our safety. This childhood trauma does not even take into
account the historical and biological trauma that we now know also

has a huge impact on how we move in this world and respond to situations. This is further exacerbated because much of our trauma response works unconsciously and, with so many of us responding with our unconscious fight, flight, freeze response, we tend to create an ongoing, never-ending loop of triggering and retriggering one another. We experience judgment and harm, often when it's not actually present, and we respond with our own judgmental thought system—all in service to greater emotional safety. This happens in families between spouses and between parents and children. It happens in our places of business between clients and customers and between colleagues. It happens among our politicians. It happens in our schools between teachers and students and among students; it is at the crux of the violence we see in our schools, and throughout society in general. Trauma is the silent and hidden cause of violence; it perpetuates passive and unconscious violence that then turns into active violence.

The antidote to trauma, and therefore the solution to violence, is CONNECTION! Most people, when they hear the word "connection," think it's an abstract concept. We all have an idea of what connection is, but it's difficult to pin down. But, thanks to my work with Nonviolent Communication (NVC), I have come to learn that connection is a replicable process that can be created with intention in all situations once people are trained and willing to work toward it. Notice I did not say it's an easy process. In fact, it may be the most difficult thing any of us ever learns—how to create connection in all situations—and yet, I can think of nothing more compelling or necessary at this stage of humanity. I think most of us can agree that we all need more connection. And I have found that this replicable process of connection is the key to reversing the trauma response. Via connection, people who have experienced trauma can attain a state of emotional safety and are less likely to respond unconsciously with fight, flight, or freeze. Furthermore, brain research shows that each time a traumatized person responds without going into fight, flight, or freeze, their neuro connections are strengthened to respond differently, and their window of tolerance gets wider. This means the more people who learn this replicable process of creating connection, the greater possibility we have of creating real, palpable peace on earth and in our individual lives.

Regarding the definition of connection at the beginning of this chapter, I see two parts. The first, this idea of ease and flow, is rather abstract, but most people seem to understand what it means because they've experienced it. **The second part of the definition is the replicable part—making sure, when we interact, that people are seen, heard, and valued without judgment.** The fact that there is a replicable process to create connection is what, I believe, can save humanity. It's the reason I'm writing this book. Connection is what NVC enables individuals to build into their interactions again and again, no matter how challenging, and this is what creates emotional safety and, thus, minimizes the unconscious fight, flight, freeze response we see everywhere around us.

In my opinion, the NVC process is miraculous because it does two things:

1. It helps move our unconscious thinking, our default mode network, into the light of day and reframe it into what is, instead of permitting a story to blindly run our reactions. This allows people to respond with more compassion toward self and others and greater effectiveness in getting their needs met.

2. It provides a communication template to use that takes the judgment out of one's thinking and language, resulting in greater safety and connection for all individuals in the interaction.

Research indicates that people who have had trauma need safety. And equal to physical safety, individuals need emotional safety to function. The National Center on Domestic Violence, Trauma and Mental Health defines emotional safety as "a state in which your innermost thoughts, feelings and experiences are, and will be, honored as one honors themselves. It's a state in which you don't need to prove, or impress; you just simply are. It's a state of openness, evenness, ease, and fluidity—with the spontaneity of a healthy child." That's a lot. I sum it up to mean that when you have emotional safety, you experience acceptance of who you are. You do not experience judgment. You can speak or act and be seen and heard fully without judgment. Because of our own trauma and our patterns of language that have been habitually modeled and handed down to us, most of us respond with judgment toward self and other without even realizing it.

"As our lives continue past the point of trauma, the amygdala is no longer reacting to real threats; rather, it is reacting *to internal voices* and perceiving them as threats, which is part of the looping stress of the DMN" (italics mine).

I included the previous sentence by Sarah Peyton in the last chapter but thought it was important to highlight again. It comes from *Your Resonant Self.*

Last chapter, I gave several examples of how this plays out for me. The looping stress of the DMN arises via external triggers in which the trauma I experienced as a child is triggered by a current-moment circumstance. These circumstances include when:

1. I perceive people as angry with me, especially when I don't see it coming.
2. I hear judgmental language directed at me or, because of lack of communication, even think someone has judgmental thoughts about me.
3. I hear judgmental language directed at others.
4. I experience that someone has more power than I do and doesn't hear me.

If you think back on Chapter 2 and the story of my growing years, and especially my interactions with my mother, you can see how these four circumstances serve as triggers to past trauma. Just yesterday, I had an interaction in which I perceived someone as angry toward me and who directed judgmental language toward me, and I didn't see it coming: "*I'm appalled by your vulgar language.*" He was referring to my use of curse words in some of my training material. I'm guessing this person had no idea that the language he chose was judgmental. (More about some of the specifics of NVC and judgmental language to come.) I'm also guessing his upset was likely triggered by his own trauma response playing out, as it usually does, unconsciously. I imagine a world where everyone becomes heightened about his own trauma and keeps from passing the baton onto others. I imagine a world where everyone knows NVC so that they can communicate fully, even when upset, and express themselves in a way where we keep one another emotionally safe and stop the cycle of epidemic trauma.

Short of moving the world in that direction, each of us has our own power, through NVC, to recover when our trauma response is set off and begins to wreak havoc on self or other. When I received that email yesterday, I noticed my insides were tense and my body felt shaky. I was scared. And that communication was still playing itself out for me internally as I wrote this piece. With the help of the NVC process, I was able to get some peaceful closure on it with myself and with the other person involved. I will use this example and others as I explain the components and subtleties of NVC so that you can better understand its power in moving toward connection and healing for self and, oftentimes, between others. Figure 6 is a description of what I did to settle internally and address the situation toward connection with the other. It will likely not mean too much to you at this point. However, I will show it to you again once I go through the NVC model and, I hope, at that point you will see how NVC works to keep all parties safe, minimize our fight, flight, freeze process, and allow us to connect more deeply and honestly with self and others.

FIGURE 6:
MY NVC PROCESS

When I received the email that contained among other things, "I'm appalled by your vulgar language," I did the following:

1. I stopped, breathed, connected to the sensation inside my body.

2. I labeled my experience with a feeling and a need. I felt scared and sad and the needs I had for myself were emotional safety, understanding, and kindness. The needs I mourned for him in the situation were sensitivity (from me) and emotional safety (for his young children who had heard my instructional video with the F word).

3. If I had any judgment about him, I kept going back and connecting with my sensations, feelings, and needs.

4. I wrote him back using only observational language and sharing the feelings and needs that surfaced. I ended with a request and an appreciation connected to my need for support, which he provided by giving me more strategies that I liked for the future.

5. I got empathy, after the fact, to keep from spiraling into judgment of self and others.

I have found that NVC, miraculously, keeps one from perpetuating blame of self or other, so we can halt the hurt and truly take peace from an abstract to a concrete working process in our world. NVC helps us to recognize our self-talk and its ties to past imprints and reroutes our thinking and actions into present-moment possibilities. I believe, if applied to scale, NVC has the power to stop the trauma epidemic that has plagued the world for generations.

WHAT IS NONVIOLENT COMMUNICATION?

Before I attempt to answer this question, I want to offer a caveat. I've heard that Marshall Rosenberg, PhD, said that he wished he hadn't written the book *Nonviolent Communication: A Language of Life*. He said this because he thought people would mistakenly think that they could do NVC by reading about it. He liked to point out that it's a process; you can learn about the process by reading, but you cannot change your language and your internal and external dialogue by digesting information. For NVC to come to life in your world, you must be committed to applying the learning. You must consistently be in the process.

Teaching and sharing NVC is my greatest joy. I think I spend 75 percent of my waking life consumed by NVC in one way or another, mostly in delight and awe. But it is a difficult thing to take hold of and scale up because it requires commitment to an outcome that will never be fully realized. Let me attempt to explain. A good friend of mine who is also one of my greatest supporters in scaling up NVC and who is also an astrophysicist said that NVC is like an asymptote.

In layman's terms, an asymptote is used in geometry to explain a goal that is only reached at infinity. For example, consider a goal that is one hundred meters away, and you can only approach it by halving your distance to the goal. In other words, the first step is fifty meters, then the second step is twenty-five meters. This strategy will reach the goal of one hundred meters, but only after an infinite number of steps. The goal of one hundred meters is an asymptote. Achieving peace via NVC is like an asymptote, in that progress gets progressively harder. Nonetheless, we make progress forward. Since the goal is only ever reached after infinite steps, the key to mastering NVC is enjoying the process, not the act of reaching the goal.

I have found that people learning NVC move between four stages on their NVC journey. Once through the first stage, a person doesn't go back, but also the fourth stage is never fully attained. At least this is the experience of my own journey and of assisting many others.

Unconsciously Unskilled

Most people start their NVC journey here. Even if they have "good" communication skills, they don't know what they don't know.

Consciously Unskilled

This is, unfortunately, where people are after reading about NVC or taking one, or even a few, introductory workshops. They learn there is this whole other way of thinking and moving in the world that has great potential, but they can't easily or frequently apply what they have learned. This is typically a very frustrating stage because people want quick outcomes, especially to painful challenges in their work and personal lives. The teachers with whom I work want to know at this stage how to transform their classroom situations so that they have greater cooperation, peace, and ease with their students. The business people with whom I work want to know how to create ongoing connections with their colleagues and reroute or minimize conflicts with clients. Parents want to know how to guide their children while maintaining a strong, loving relationship. In all of these circumstances, people have real-world, pressing challenges in the moment and want solutions as quickly as possible. Also, I have found that most people are busy, very busy and very overwhelmed. The overwhelm is oftentimes and ironically due to their interaction processes, and their busyness often keeps them from committing to the process, which is the solution. What is hard to convey is that the process *is* the solution. There is no finish line, no point where you'll say, "I'm finally there."

Consciously Skilled

By staying *in* the process continually, individuals begin to have greater awareness of their thinking and language, and they begin to apply the hard but replicable processes for greater connection in their lives. I have found that people need to stay consciously *in* the process for a long time before seeing glimpses of the next stage. And what do I mean by *in* the process? I think individuals begin to get consciously skilled best by attending regular NVC practice groups; weekly is ideal. Another way to become consciously skilled is by surrounding oneself with people who intentionally use NVC process in their conversations and meetings. Both of these scenarios require individuals being in a conscious NVC community where they are encouraged to work on their inner and outer conversations, their self-talk, and their interpersonal conversations.

Unconsciously Skilled

Eventually, some of the NVC skills and distinctions begin to replace old habits of mind and interactions. The more individuals stay in practice and/or in NVC community, the more reinforcement they get, eventually, for doing the hard, time-consuming work, and the more the skills become more automatic and relatively easier.

There is no fast path to nirvana! NVC is not learned via intellectual understanding. It's an iterative process that one attains by staying engaged. It's an iterative process that grows you immediately as you use it, but you must use it to evolve your skills and you must build in support structures and time to ensure that you keep at it. The time factor seems to be a conundrum; we don't have it, and our poor communications and interactions end up feeding the frenzy that limits our time and our minds. I've found it to be one of those counterintuitive things, kind of like meditation. We don't have time, but if we can make it a priority, it gives us our life and our time back. I constantly come back to the thought, *Is there anything more important than having connection with ourselves and the people in our lives?* If your answer to that is no, then I beg of you to learn and put forth the time to own the NVC process.

Now onto the process itself. I usually take eight weeks to introduce NVC to my students. Check out The Bigbie Method at www.thebigbiemethod.com where you can learn more about our training and certification. In the next part of this chapter, I will attempt to hit the highlights of the NVC process and show you how each of these components/processes is connected to rerouting our faulty default mode networks (self-talk) and providing means for keeping all parties emotionally safe in our communications, even in tough interactions.

Remember, Nonviolent Communication is a process to use when one wants connection. Connection is the flow and ease that occurs within and between people when they experience being seen, heard, and valued without judgment. It takes work to make connection, especially in conflict. So, please note, you may not choose to use NVC in all situations. But, if you do, here is an explanation of how it works.

I'm providing the details of NVC here to whet your whistle, to give you basic knowledge of the process and its various components, and to explain why it works to reroute our trauma response and can, therefore, help reverse the trauma epidemic we have on hand.

THE NVC TEMPLATE

Figure 7 shows what I call the NVC Dance Floor. At the beginning stage of your learning, it is likely overwhelming and confusing when you look at it. I want to give you the complete picture here so you can see the various components and to plant the seed that there are many concepts and skills that go into it. Looking under the microscope, each box and each vertical section are a lesson unto themselves. Don't worry if it doesn't make sense. For now, just know that there is a template and there are many pieces to learn and put together.

Figure 7: The NVC Dance Floor

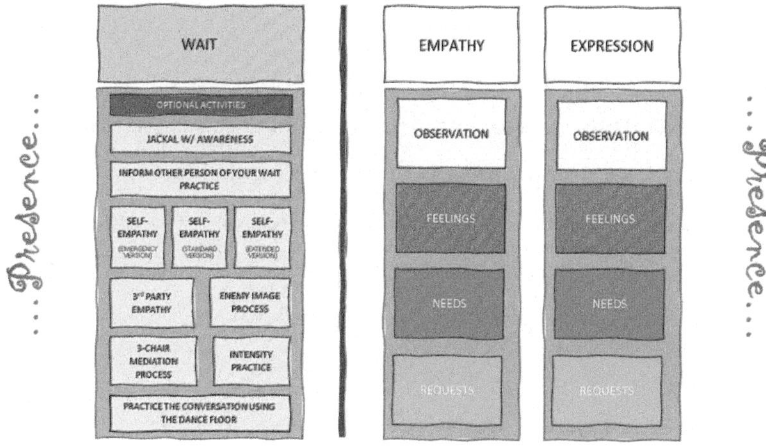

Please refer to Appendix B for a larger version.

Figure 8 shows a more simplified version of the Dance Floor. Zooming out to look at it in this way, you see three major concepts: Empathy, Expression, and WAIT. The interplay of these concepts is also a major learning for users. Simplified, NVC is like a dance in which you move back and forth between these three concepts. We will go more into detail about what is meant by empathy, but for now know that it is usually easiest to create connection if you can start with empathy of self and other first. If you can create an interaction where the other person experiences being heard and valued without judgment, then when you express yourself there is a much greater chance that you will be heard as well. Sounds simple, but remember, most of us respond with our fight, flight, freeze reaction in conflict and find it near impossible to get present enough to hear another without judgment. If this occurs, it's a signal to move to the WAIT portion of the Dance Floor. WAIT in NVC stands for "Why Am I Talking?" or "What Am I Thinking?" It is *not* just a cool-down time; it is an active time where the individual uses several processes to shift their energy and thinking so that they can step back over to empathy for the other individual and try the conversation again. This is the bird's-eye view of NVC and how it ideally works. There may be times when one starts with WAIT or Expression, but Empathy first seems to be ideal.

Figure 8: The NVC Dance Floor Simplified

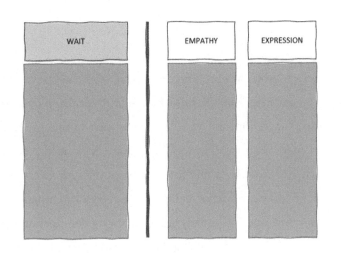

Please refer to Appendix B for a larger version.

> "The significant problems we face cannot be solved
> at the same level of thinking that created them."
> —ALBERT EINSTEIN

When teaching this sequence in workshops, I often share Einstein's quote. After all, to use this process we must respond in a completely different way than how we have been trained for thousands of years. We must literally reroute our brain's response and move from the amygdala (fight, flight, freeze) to our prefrontal cortex—the thinking part of our brain. If we find we can't give empathy first, it's likely because we, ourselves, need deep resonance or empathy first to connect with what was triggered in the situation. We need to make sense of our trigger in terms of our need(s) and give presence to the associated sensations (what is alive) so that, even at a cellular level, we integrate the aroused sensations and settle back to a state of equanimity. By getting empathy from a third party or giving ourselves empathy, when we are aroused and unable to give it to the other person in the conflict, we integrate our thinking and our bodily reaction in a way that brings about a sense of safety and/or deep resolution. This allows one to move from the amygdala (alarm system) to the prefrontal cortex (reasoning, problem-solving, comprehension, impulse control, creativity, and perseverance). This is why the WAIT portion of the Dance Floor is vital and active. It is the place where we can reach down into our needs, our DMN. It allows us to separate our story from what is, and process what is, so that we are not so bound up by it and have greater ability to speak with clarity, free of judgment.

WHAT IS EMPATHY?

When teaching empathy, I get concerned that most individuals new to NVC think they already know what it is. They come to the learning with a preformed mental model of the word. A colleague of mine used to joke that we need to make up a whole different word, "empiathy," so that individuals would understand we are talking about something different than their preformed notion.

At The Bigbie Method, we teach that NVC empathy has three components that weave together: presence, reflection, and needs guesses. Let's go over each of these briefly.

Presence

By this we mean putting your full attention on another (or in self-empathy on yourself). Sounds simple enough, but when learning NVC, most people begin to get a greater understanding of their squirrely mind. Our minds seem to be habituated to being caught up in our thoughts. This is especially true when we are in conflict, and our thinking mind literally takes us out of presence. Our default mode network kicks in, usually unconsciously, with blame of self and other, and then a network of thoughts start in an attempt to move our internal experience to safety. It's no surprise that staying fully present is a task. So, much like with meditation, getting present in our communication requires practice and intent. When you slip out of it, it requires noticing and then bringing yourself back to fully being with the other (or with self-empathy being fully with yourself).

Reflection

If NVC is used toward connection—and connection is created when people experience being seen, heard, and valued—then reflection can be very helpful to create connection. Reflection is literally repeating back or, better yet, paraphrasing what you heard the other person say. It is used to close the loop for the person speaking and the person listening to ensure that the message sent was received in the way intended. This is a missing piece in our conversations that, often, leads to misunderstanding and disconnection. I frequently joke that people tell one another, "Yeah, I understand," and then go on with the conversation in a way that reveals otherwise. Also, without this message sent/message received feedback loop, the individual speaking may tend to fill in stories of what he thinks the other person understands or doesn't. The speaker may also make up stories about the listener's reaction to what was said. This is where a damaged default mode network can begin to wreak havoc. There is so much room for misinterpretation. Reflecting helps to minimize one's faulty stories. Reflecting gives the party speaking a sense of being heard. It is a way for the listener to convey understanding without necessarily agreeing.

Needs Guesses

Please pay attention here because I'm about to share the #1 principle of NVC. *All conflict is a tragic expression of an unmet need.* By need, I mean the abstract concepts that all individuals want in their lives. Figure 9 is a list of Universal Human Needs. Think of any conflict you have in your life and you can ultimately trace it back to one or several of these needs. However, when we are in conflict, we rarely understand the needs in play, so we certainly cannot express them easily. Instead, most of us attempt to communicate strategies to meet our needs, and conflict and disconnection ensue.

Figure 9: Universal Human Needs

WELL BEING	EXPRESSION	CONNECTION
Sustenance/Health	Autonomy/Authenticity	Love/Caring
abundance, thriving	choice	affection
exercise	congruence	closeness
food/nutrition	consistency	companionship
rest, sleep	continuity	compassion
sustainability	dignity	intimacy
support, help	freedom	kindness
survival	honesty	mattering, importance
wellness	independence	nurturing
	initiative	partnership
Safety/Security	innovation	presence
comfort	integrity	sexual connection
confidence	power	touch
emotional safety	transparency	warmth
familiarity	openness	
order, structure	wholeness	Empathy/Understanding
predictability		awareness
protection from harm	Creativity/Play	clarity
relaxation	adventure	communication
self-esteem	discovery	consideration
shelter	fun	hearing (hear/be heard)
stability	humor	knowing (know/be known)
trust	inspiration	presence
	joy	respect
Peace/Beauty/Rest	movement	seeing (see/be seen)
acceptance	passion	sensitivity
appreciation, gratitude	spontaneity	
awareness		Community/Belonging
balance	Meaning/Contribution	cooperation
clarity	aliveness	equality
ease	achievement, productivity	fellowship
equanimity	celebration/mourning	inclusion
harmony	challenge	interdependence
presence	competence	harmony
recreation	efficacy	mutuality
relaxation	effectiveness	reciprocity
simplicity	feedback	solidarity
space	growth	support
tranquility	learning, clarity	trust
wonder	mystery	
	participation	
	purpose, value	

John Kinyon — www.mediateyourlife.com

Please refer to Appendix B for a larger version.

In NVC, there is a key distinction between a need and a strategy. Needs are universal; they are what all human beings want, and strategies are individualized ways of getting our needs met. When we fight, we usually fight at a strategy level with little knowledge of the needs at hand. For instance, a couple might have an argument about someone "staying out late with his friends" and not talk about the needs at hand. For the person going out, needs might include fun and relaxation; for the person who is upset, the needs could be inclusion, mattering, and connection. No one taught us to identify and communicate our needs. In fact, in our society, just the word "need" is often frowned upon, probably because of associations with "being needy"—which is a judgment. (More to come on that.)

So, a key part of NVC empathy is taking needs guesses. "Are you needing (fill in a need)?" or "Is this about (fill in a need)?" Notice we are taking a guess, not making a declarative statement. Giving empathy requires curiosity, a leaning in to understand what is at hand. In so doing, the person receiving the presence, reflection, and needs guesses is guided to greater presence of self and greater emotional safety with other. Also, as we will learn in subsequent sections, we pair this empathy with a very conscious choice of language that removes blame and judgment from the interaction. Together, empathy and judgment-free communication ensures connection.

Notice by using these three components only, the person giving empathy is steered away from using what I call "Other Conversational Responses," which oftentimes have judgment (either consciously or unconsciously) and/or can guide the communication away from the person speaking. Notice how both instances (turning the conversation in a different direction or using judgments) move individuals away from the definition of connection: being seen, heard, and valued without judgment. NVC empathy à la presence, reflection, and needs guesses tends to give the person speaking a sense of connection. By using presence, reflection, and needs guesses, you literally create a replicable process of seeing, hearing, and valuing without judgment.

In many ways, the NVC empathy process is a game changer when it comes to trauma. It seems to be the missing component for individuals after a traumatic event or circumstance. Remember earlier when you read about the connection between how one is received after trauma and whether they do or don't carry that trauma forward in future years? Being heard and deeply known around the needs you are mourning because of the painful event is essential to keeping the trauma from replaying going forward. Oftentimes, pain and faulty thinking persist because the traumatized individual doesn't get support to connect them back up to the rest of the brain and make sense of the event. So, if more individuals were held with empathy after a difficult event, it would minimize their brain's tendency to flip into survival mode going forward. The brain could compartmentalize what happened (the Observation) put the Feelings and Needs in their proper place.

If more people enlisted the NVC empathy process during a conflict and/or in their everyday communication process—at work, in school, at home—there would be less misinterpretation and misunderstanding and less DMN story-making which would equate to less inner and interpersonal conflict and more connection. I saw evidence of this at the local RJ program I ran with youth that others found difficult to reach and difficult to help reroute their fight, flight, freeze response. Youth with a tendency to fight and shut down did not have those behaviors in the program because this NVC empathy process was the backbone of all that we did. Also, there was conscious use of Other Conversational Responses when we chose to use such responses instead of empathy. Most of the communications we had were intentionally in service to connection—making sure the teens were seen, heard, and valued without judgment. Consequently, there was little room for story-making and misinterpretations and, therefore, greater emotional safety and less trauma triggers in play. We intentionally created connection!

OTHER CONVERSATIONAL RESPONSES

So, what do I mean by Other Conversational Responses, and how do they differ from empathy? Whether we are in a conflict or just talking to someone in a more neutral situation, we all have a variety of responses that we use. Many of these responses are habitual patterns that we use unconsciously in certain circumstances. Figure 10 shows many such responses. The responses indicated are clustered in a specific manner. The first and second columns are responses we tend to use when we are in a neutral conversation. For example, a friend comes to us to share about a problem or circumstance in their life. In this situation, we might give advice or relate or sympathize or any of the other replies listed in columns 1 and 2.

However, sometimes we are *in* a conflict with someone. And in those circumstances, most people would draw from columns 2 or 3 for their retort. When in the fight, we tend to shut down the other, joke, explain, correct, threaten, or any of the other options in columns 2 and 3.

Figure 10: Other Conversational Responses

When the other person is in conflict with someone else (not you)...	When the other person is in conflict with someone else or you are in conflict with each other...	When you are in conflict with each other...
We tend to...	We tend to...	We tend to...
• Agree	• Give advice	• Threaten other
• Relate	• Minimize	• Correct other
• One up	• Shut down	• Explain to other
• Devil's advocate	• Joke	• Evaluate other
• Sympathize	• Ask questions	• Criticize other
• Commiserate	• Comment	• Blame other
• Champion	• Explain	

Please refer to Appendix B for a larger version.

There is nothing inherently "wrong" with many of these responses. I find I still use many of the possibilities from columns 1 and 2 in my interactions. But once we learn NVC process, we find we have more intentionality in the responses we use. First, we learn to ask before we respond. "Are you open to some advice?" "Can I relate for a second?" "Do you want to hear an explanation?" Also, we choose our responses more with a specific guide of connection and less out of unconscious habit. This is helpful because, oftentimes, our habitual responses create more disconnection. We say something in service to getting through a conflict and/or protecting ourselves in the conflict, or, in a neutral situation, we say something to make a friend feel better, but things tend to get worse. Often, we are baffled as to where things went south. If we were to look at each of these response possibilities with a critical eye on how they measure up to the definition of connection provided earlier, we would see that many of these responses fall short of that definition. (See Figure 11.)

It's relatively easy to see why many of the options in column 3 would cause disconnection, but what about the options in columns 1 and 2? Let's think about how giving advice might not fit the definition of connection. After all, most people giving advice have an intention to help, right? However, please note that if you give someone advice, you are basically saying that something is not okay and needs to change. Remember, people who have trauma need emotional safety, they need to know they are okay just as they are. So, if you give someone advice (especially if it's unsolicited), you may notice that it is not received well. Giving advice doesn't line up with the definition of connection because there is inherent judgment in advice-giving. Relating is another response that many people use, especially in a neutral situation with a friend or loved one. It's used to connect, to let the other know, "I feel you." Unfortunately, at times it backfires. Why? Because if connection occurs when people experience being seen, heard, and valued, then a person who relates is turning the conversation in the other direction, on themselves, and the person who was sharing may not experience being heard or seen or valued.

I want to reiterate. There is nothing inherently "wrong" with giving advice or relating or many of these other responses—but are you responding out of habit or in greatest service to connection in the moment? Here is one more example. You get into an argument with your significant other about being late to the ballfield. You immediately launch into an explanation of why you were late, hoping for some understanding and resolution to the disconnection. However, the other person doesn't want to hear it and keeps going with their onslaught. Why didn't the explanation bring resolution? Because all conflict is about an unmet need. Before you provide the explanation, your significant other needs connection around the need(s) that was triggered for them. It's likely that their fight, flight, freeze is triggered in that moment, and having an understanding and acknowledgment of the need in play allows the person to connect to the prefrontal cortex and come back to presence and, likely, a greater ability to hear your explanation. Therefore, empathy (through presence, reflection, and needs guesses) is usually extremely helpful first, before you launch into an explanation.

Figure 11: Other Conversational Responses
Compared to Connection Definition

Please refer to Appendix B for a larger version.

NVC EXPRESSION

While empathy is a key component of NVC, expression is equally valuable and, oftentimes, not as obvious within the process. However, if you revisit the NVC Dance Floor, you will see that the expression line is as prominent as the empathy line. It's a wonderful ideology and practice to hear others deeply. However, if the equation is lopsided, then connection suffers. Remember the definition of connection? The ease and flow that occurs within and between people when they are seen, heard, and valued without judgment. If one person consistently has this in a relationship and the other person does not, the connection between them will likely diminish.

The problem with most traditional expression is that most people have no idea when judgment goes through their minds and out of their mouths. Also, we lean heavily on those Other Conversational Responses in our communications, so when we go to express, oftentimes, we become more distant from the people in our lives. Starting with empathy for the other first can, oftentimes, open the door to being able to express. Additionally, in NVC, we learn a way of expressing that can keep judgment out of the communication and further allow the other to hear one's message. Relating this back to trauma, if we can keep our language and our hearts and minds free of judgment, then the person receiving our message will experience safety and be less likely to react with fight, flight, freeze.

Getting one's message to be free of judgment can help the messenger as well. In so doing, they can step out of their default mode network—the unconscious talking going on in their mind—and into what is actually going on in the present moment. To do this, it's important to look at the Dance Floor again and notice the boxes under both Expression and Empathy: Observations, Feelings, Needs, and Requests, also known as OFNR. When we can hear with OFNR and express with OFNR, we are able to keep blame and judgment out of our interactions and provide intentional emotional safety for all.

I consider OFNR to be our NVC training wheels. When first learning to ride a bike, we need those training wheels. They give us support but also feel quite wobbly, and they are definitely not cool. Once you have mastered riding the bike, you take them off and, with additional guidance, you are able to fly. Remember the freedom of your first ride without training wheels? NVC OFNR is similar. It's helpful for people to understand and make the distinctions between OFNR and their opposites. And, when people first start talking with the training wheels, it's clunky and uncomfortable and not cool! But, with practice and guidance, it becomes easier, smoother, and it can help you fly to greater and more connecting heights in your communications.

As mentioned above, OFNR stands for Observations, Feelings, Needs, and Requests. Let's talk about each one of them here.

OBSERVATIONS VERSUS EVALUATIONS

Figure 12: Observation on the NVC Dance Floor

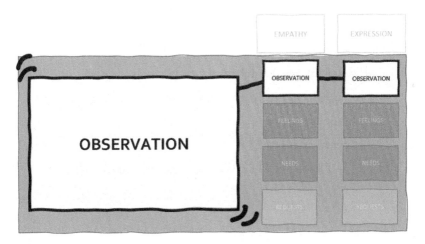

Please refer to Appendix B for a larger version.

The yellow color in the Observation box indicates shining a light, being able to see (Figure 12). Whether giving empathy or expressing, in NVC individuals are guided to put things in observational terms as opposed to evaluating or interpreting. At first blush, this seems straightforward enough, but when applied, most people find it difficult and enlightening. What is the difference between observations and evaluations? Observations are what we can directly see, hear, smell, taste, and/or feel through touch. Evaluations are the thoughts and interpretations in our minds that get triggered by an observation. For example, saying, "You are disrespectful and out of control" contains evaluation. Believe it or not, you can't see someone being disrespectful or out of control. You can hear someone saying "fuck you" and see someone punching the wall three times, and then you might have the evaluative thoughts that the person is disrespectful and out of control. In NVC, we find it to be helpful to stick with the observation and leave the judgments/evaluations out of the conversation. For example, I heard you say "fuck you" and then you hit the wall three times with your fist.

It's especially useful to stick with observations when in an argument—for several reasons.

- ▸ Evaluations can complicate, muddy, and exacerbate the topic about which you are fighting. Observations are the facts; you're not adding in your emotions or your feelings or your opinions and interpretations. Evaluations are the opinions and interpretations. For example, what is "yelling" to one person because of their family or culture might not be yelling to another person. So, when you add in these evaluations, you can start a whole other argument about the evaluations and whether they're valid or not, whether they are factual or not, whether you agree or not, and so on, and the original issue becomes lost and unresolved. "I didn't yell. I don't know what you are talking about." Evaluations tend to escalate and complicate things.
- ▸ Evaluations create negative feelings for the person saying them and the person receiving them. If you were to stop and self-connect (breathe and notice your internal sensations) amid communicating an evaluation, you would probably notice feeling a lot of the things on the

very bottom of the Feelings list (Figure 14), because evaluations tend to make us angry. Thoughts often lead to a whole other level of suffering. At the brain level, our DMN goes into blame mode because it's the unconscious script that was handed to us, and the amygdala kicks in to keep us safe by blaming or fighting back. Then we make something fundamentally wrong about the other so, therefore, we are okay. "It's them, they are the problem." And then the other will likely respond with their fight, flight, freeze response, and on and on it goes. My mother defaulted to making unconscious judgmental comments about and toward those with whom she was in conflict. In her primary relationships, this unconscious protective response was the cause of much disconnection, dishar-mony, and angst. It took her a lifetime to understand this was in play in her relationships and in our relationship, but in the end, thanks to NVC, she really understood and regretted the damage it had caused between us. More on that in Chapter 5.

▶ Observations help the communication/connection flow between you and the other person. There's a place to start upon which you can agree.

▶ Observations take a lot of heat out of your own internal dialogue. In other words, observations help a person move out of a faulty DMN and operate with the facts in the circumstance.

THOUGHTS VERSUS FEELINGS

Figure 13: Feelings on the NVC Dance Floor

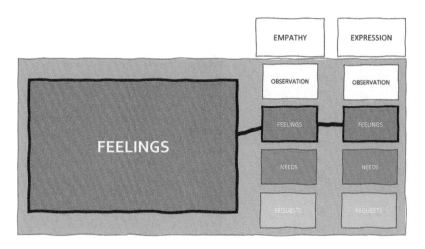

Please refer to Appendix B for a larger version.

The red color in the Feelings box represents the heart or fire of feelings (Figure 13). Have you ever felt ignored? Most people would respond with yes to this question. However, in NVC, feeling ignored is not considered a feeling. It's a thought; you think someone is ignoring you. Most of us get these two internal processes confused. Feelings are internal states, sensations in our bodies. Thoughts are the things that go on in our heads, things we tell ourselves in our heads. At The Bigbie Method (TBM), we guide people to contemplating the list shown to help determine their feelings. If you think someone is ignoring you, how might you feel? Look at the list (Figure 14).

Figure 14: Universal Human Feelings

PEACEFUL	LOVING	GLAD	PLAYFUL	INTERESTED
tranquil	warm	happy	energetic	involved
calm	affectionate	excited	effervescent	inquisitive
content	tender	hopeful	invigorated	intense
engrossed	appreciative	joyful	zestful	enriched
absorbed	friendly	satisfied	refreshed	absorbed
expansive	sensitive	delighted	impish	alert
serene	compassionate	encouraged	alive	aroused
loving	grateful	grateful	lively	astonished
blissful	nurtured	confident	exuberant	concerned
satisfied	amorous	inspired	giddy	curious
relaxed	trusting	touched	adventurous	eager
relieved	open	proud	mischievous	enthusiastic
quiet	thankful	exhilarated	jubilant	fascinated
carefree	radiant	ecstatic	goofy	intrigued
composed	adoring	optimistic	buoyant	surprised
fulfilled	passionate	glorious	electrified	helpful

MAD	SAD	SCARED	TIRED	CONFUSED
impatient	lonely	afraid	exhausted	frustrated
pessimistic	heavy	fearful	fatigued	perplexed
disgruntled	troubled	terrified	inert	hesitant
frustrated	helpless	startled	lethargic	troubled
irritable	gloomy	nervous	indifferent	uncomfortable
edgy	overwhelmed	jittery	weary	withdrawn
grouchy	distant	horrified	overwhelmed	apathetic
agitated	despondent	anxious	fidgety	embarrassed
exasperated	discouraged	worried	helpless	hurt
disgusted	distressed	anguished	heavy	uneasy
irked	dismayed	lonely	sleepy	irritated
cantankerous	disheartened	insecure	disinterested	suspicious
animosity	despairing	sensitive	reluctant	unsteady
bitter	sorrowful	shocked	passive	puzzled
rancorous	unhappy	apprehensive	dull	restless
irate, furious	depressed	dread	bored	boggled
angry	blue	jealous	listless	chagrined
hostile	miserable	desperate	blah	unglued
enraged	dejected	suspicious	mopey	detached
violent	melancholy	frightened	comatose	skeptical

John Kinyon – www.mediateyourlife.com

Please refer to Appendix B for a larger version.

You might feel sad or angry or any number of other emotions. When we say, "I feel ignored," we aren't stating a feeling. Ignored is not a feeling, it's a judgmental thought that is disguised as a feeling; we are sticking the word "feeling" in front of a judgmental thought.

We are really trying to say, "I think you are ignoring me." This is a big "aha" for many folks. We don't realize how many times we say, "I feel…" and what comes after is not a feeling—it's a faux feeling, a judgmental thought. In fact, we do this quite often and without realizing it. Here I've provided a list of common words we tend to mix up as feelings but are thoughts/judgments and are likely causing a lot of grief out there. The list is not complete but will give you an idea of these "thought feelings" or "faux feelings."

Ignored	Overworked	Taken for granted
Left out	Patronized	Trapped
Insulted	Powerless	Threatened
Interrupted	Pressured	Tricked
Invalidated	Provoked	Unappreciated
Isolated	Put down	Unloved
Manipulated	Rejected	Unwanted
Mistrusted	Ripped off	Used
Misunderstood	Screwed	Victimized
Neglected	Smothered	Wronged

In NVC, pure feelings do not include those which involve another person. If you say, "I feel abandoned," it involves another person to abandon you, so that's not a feeling, it's a judgmental, blaming thought disguised as a feeling. You are really blaming the other person for doing something to you. And, by the way, the person hearing "I feel abandoned" will likely get upset because they will hear it as the judgment it really is. To lessen the likelihood of further disconnection, in NVC, we attempt to stick with pure observations and state our feelings as our feelings and own our thoughts as our thoughts and then (as will be shown in the next section) state our needs. Translating "I feel abandoned" into something like, "When you went to the party without me (Observation), I was sad and angry (Feelings), and I was mourning inclusion (Needs)." The person will still likely not enjoy that message, but it will allow for greater understanding and connection because you are keeping the communication clean of judgments. Remember connection occurs when people are seen, heard, and valued without judgment.

People also tend to say, "I feel like..." or "I feel that..." and I guarantee what follows is not a feeling but a thought. "I feel like you don't listen to anything I say." That is not a feeling, it's a thought, a judgment. "I feel that July is the best month of the year." Again, that is not a feeling; it's a thought. On and on and on...this misuse of "feel" is deeply embedded in how we communicate with one another. So, what's the big deal?

Sometimes I feel like I'm the feelings/thoughts Nazi-judge! Do you see the irony of that sentence? Just to hammer it home one more time, I don't *feel* that way—it's not a feeling, it's a thought. And, yes, sometimes I do think that I go overboard with this distinction, but I think it can be toxic when the two concepts are unconsciously confused and used, and I think most people end up with greater mental health and clarity when they begin to use the concepts true to form.

Just like with distinguishing between observations and evaluations, distinguishing between feelings and thoughts can have a great impact on our communications directly between people and, also, regarding the inner dialogue that, often, feeds our communication process. When we can share our true feelings, void of judgment, the other person is usually more open because he, too, experiences those feelings. They can understand you without being triggered into a fight, flight, freeze response. They might not enjoy what you share, but they are more apt to take it in, lean into what you are attempting to communicate.

The other huge benefit to getting clear and communicating feelings as feelings and thoughts as thoughts is that it allows us to have greater clarity on our inner dialogue and to begin to see when we make stuff up. I have found that this is a game changer, especially for people who suffer from mental health issues like anxiety and depression—which is many of us! The default mode network is ushered out of the shadow into the light of day. And when we can see our thoughts as thoughts and then tie them to the observation, and to what we are feeling and needing, we have greater clarity and ease internally and a much better ability to communicate our needs while keeping the other party safe.

NEEDS VERSUS STRATEGIES

Figure 15: Needs on the NVC Dance Floor

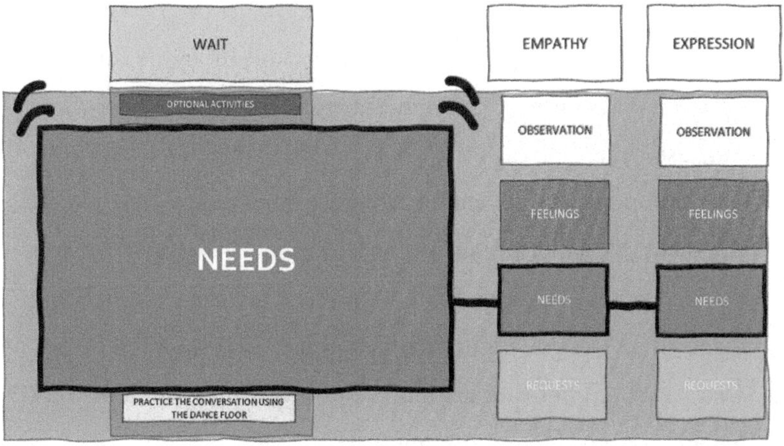

Please refer to Appendix B for a larger version.

The blue color in the Needs box represents the universality of needs. Earlier, we mentioned the main idea on which NVC is based, that "all conflict is a tragic expression of an unmet need." As we revealed previously, the NVC empathy process is based largely on sourcing the Universal Human Need(s) in play. As we can see in Figure 15, needs are a critical component whether giving empathy to other or expressing one's own truth. In conflict, we often are not even aware of the underlying needs, and we tend to speak at a strategy level. We argue about someone cleaning up the clothes all over the floor (strategy) without even mentioning some of the needs in play like order, consideration, rest, cooperation, partnership. I'm naming a few needs here, but there could be others. NVC differentiates between needs and strategies. Needs are abstract concepts that everyone in the world desires, and strategies are individualized ways of getting our needs met. There are many ways to get our needs met, but we often get stuck in one strategy, which escalates the conflict.

Using needs, whether in empathy or expressing, is useful in minimizing the fight, flight, freeze response that people typically display in conflict for at least two reasons.

1. It helps in the dialogue to create a place where people can start to hear one another. Since we all share the same needs, if we can communicate them along with the specific observation and feelings, then we have a much greater ability to create common ground upon which to start the conversation. Also, since all people share the same needs, there is often more ability to understand and care when someone expresses their needs or when needs are unearthed during empathy or listening.

2. At a brain level, identifying needs moves the brain's functioning into the prefrontal cortex and allows one to see the bigger picture. Identifying the deep longings that are at play moves us into the self-regulation skill of reframing. In other words, getting connected to one's needs literally moves a person from the amygdala into the higher-level thinking part of the brain.

So, NVC works its magic in two ways. It helps to bring people together in their communications by creating connection through processes that support people in being seen, heard, and valued without judgment. And it provides a specific template for individuals to reroute their brain's survival response.

Researchers have found that brains find their way back to emotional balance in three main ways:

1. Identifying what we are feeling (naming emotions).
2. Thinking about the situation in a different way (reframing).
3. Thinking about something else instead of what is bothering us (distraction).

The NVC process we have shared here works to minimize fight, flight, freeze internally and between people because it hits on all three. In addition to the internal benefits, stating things in Observation, Feelings, and Needs, instead of with evaluation, aids in emotional safety for everyone involved in the communication as well.

University of Virginia researcher, James Coan, has added one more piece to the puzzle of how brains return to calm: the real or imagined presence of a person who cares about us (accompaniment). When he says accompaniment or cares about us, he means something akin to the empathy process explained previously, which is foundational to NVC. Remember my experience of the RJ program's teens looking different after just five minutes of receiving empathy? I always had a hunch that something was going on in their brains to cause the difference in outward appearance.

When in a dialogue with NVC as the framework, we use the Observations, Feelings, and Needs while listening and speaking and, in so doing, this allows for a replicable experience of connection (being seen, heard, and valued without judgment.) But there is one more piece to the NVC Dance Floor: Requests.

REQUESTS VERSUS DEMANDS

Figure 16: Requests on the NVC Dance Floor

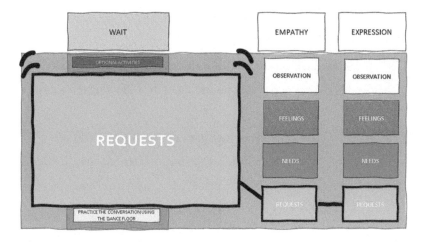

Please refer to Appendix B for a larger version.

The green color in the Requests box (Figure 16) represents Go! In NVC, we make the distinction between a request and a demand and attempt to use requests in lieu of demands whenever possible. The difference between the two is simple in concept but, like much of the NVC process, difficult in execution. When asking something of self or other, we try to remain open to all possibilities, and if the other person says no for any reason, nothing is diminished in the relationship; we don't get mad. If a person says no, it merely cycles us back into the NVC empathy process, and we become curious regarding the "need behind the no." Except for asking to engage in a dialogue, which comes at the beginning of the Dance Floor process and is not represented in Figure 16, most Requests in the NVC model come after the Observation, Feeling, and Need (for other à la empathy or for self à la expression) are stated. Before you make a request, one way to determine if your ask is a request or demand is to check your gut. If you have a lot of emotion tied up with your ask and you sense that you will be angry if you don't get what you want, then you are likely about to make a demand. Robert Gonzalez, a beloved NVC trainer, puts it pointedly in the following quotation.

"One of the biggest obstacles in the practice
of compassionate communication is when I am attached to
having a particular outcome to a particular need met.
I feel it in the body as a kind of 'have to have.'
We might not use those words, but it is the energy that
communicates. The energy is often a feeling
of desperation or urgency."

–ROBERT GONZALES

Marshall Rosenberg also had some wisdom to share about this distinction. He said, "Making requests is premised on the radical understanding that if something works for us and not for another, we pay a price that is too dear." Remember the definition of connection? The flow and ease that occurs within and between people when they experience being seen, heard, and valued without judgment. There is an inherent judgment when one makes a demand: "Something is not okay. You are not okay." And therefore, the price we pay in making it is our connection with the other (or self if making a demand of self.) We literally are cut off from the need underneath. If we can return to the need of self or other, we have the potential of taking the heat out of the ask and moving it into the territory of a request. Another famous Marshall quotation is that "a negotiable request gives the other person the opportunity to contribute to our life with joy, not because they 'have to' or 'should,' or out of guilt, shame, or fear of punishment if they say 'no.'" A request, by definition, can be refused.

If you notice that your ask is with demand energy, it is a clear indication that you likely need empathy around it. You need to get connected deeply to the underlying need and process the need so that you can make an ask without an attachment to outcome. In NVC, we do this by getting empathy from a third-party person or by a process we call self-empathy. I will touch, briefly, on the self-empathy process in the WAIT section to follow.

One more general point about requests: you can keep asking them. Kind of like a dog that nudges your hand when asking to be rubbed and continues to do so if you stop rubbing. You get drawn into rubbing him because of the way he asks, with the gentle, persistent, and sweet nudge that tugs at your heart. You're open to contributing to his need. You, too, can "dog for your needs." You can keep asking the person, but do you ask with urgency or underlying anger or guilt, or is the ask more of a gentle nudge while expressing your need?

In NVC, we use two different kinds of Requests: Connecting Requests and Action Requests (Figure 17).

CONNECTING REQUESTS VERSUS ACTION REQUESTS

Figure 17: Connecting Requests & Action Requests

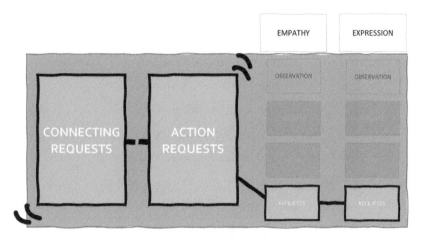

Please refer to Appendix B for a larger version.

Connecting Requests are so important, and yet they seem to be the thing we've never learned to insert into our communications, especially during conflicts. Connecting Requests usually come before we enter a dialogue or before we express or after we have given empathy or expressed (via Observation, Feelings, Needs) and we want to make sure that the other person was heard or that we were heard in the way intended. You state Observations (by saying what you are seeing or hearing) and taking Feeling and Needs guesses of what's going on with other or expressing your own Feelings and Needs and then make a Connecting Request to make sure the needs were sourced and understood.

Connecting Requests are important for several reasons:

- They promote a high quality of connection and trust between two people. They help ensure that each person has the experience of being seen, heard, and valued, creating the experience of: *I'm hearing your needs, you're hearing my needs. Okay. We're connected, we get each other.* It creates the understanding and trust between each party that you care about each other's needs.

- They help move us from one area of the NVC Dance Floor to the other, to make sure everyone is self-connected, clear, and calm, that everyone expresses and is listened to and understood.

- They help ensure presence, willingness, and participation.

- They come before and help set the stage for Action Requests (which are requests to do something differently going forward, or suggestion of a strategy). Connecting Requests help bring greater clarity regarding each person's needs, and therefore increase the likelihood of generating solutions that meet everyone's needs.

In Figure 18, I provide a list of the three types of Connecting Requests and some examples. They are categorized by what they are requesting.

1. Request for Dialogue

This request is asking if the other person is open and available for the communication. We tend to launch right into our communications without ensuring that it's a good time for the other. The simple practice of asking, "Hey, can we talk about what happened?" can make all the difference in how the conversation goes. It creates greater emotional safety right from the beginning of an interaction because you are making sure the other person has a choice and is resourced for the conversation.

2. Request for Empathy

This request can be used when giving empathy to other to make sure you are on track with what's going on for the other, in terms of his needs. Say you just used your OFN training wheels, "So, when you left the dishes in the sink last night (O), I'm wondering if you were just really tired (F) and you would like some understanding (N) about that." You could end with "Is that right?" or "Am I on track with your needs around that?" That's the Connecting Request.

You could also use this kind of Connecting Request for empathy if you express and you want to ensure that the other person is hearing you in the way you would like. This is a great way to get the other person to give empathy, even if they have never taken an NVC class. Either before or after you state your OFN, "When I saw the dishes in the sink this morning (O), I was exhausted and frustrated (F) and was sad (F) about cooperation and support (N)." You can make the Connecting Request, "I'd love to know if you get the feelings and needs I'm trying to express?" In this way, you are gently guiding the other person to connect with your needs.

3. Request for Expression

This Connecting Request can be used after you have given the other person empathy and connected around their needs. You can then request to be heard about your experience. "Thanks for sharing. Do you mind if I say a few words next?" So, rather than just launching into what you want to say, again you check for the availability of the other. Even working with some of the "toughest" kids, I have found that most people are much more open to hearing what you want to say after they have been heard and when you give the courtesy of making sure they are emotionally available to take in what you'd like to share.

Another way the request for expression is used in the NVC model is after you have expressed and stated your OFN, you ask how that was for the other person to hear. For instance, say you said, "When I saw the dishes in the sink this morning (O), I was exhausted and frustrated (F) and was sad (F) about cooperation and support (N). I'd love to know if you get the feelings and needs I'm trying to express?" And say the other person shares back your feelings and needs. Then it might be fruitful to ask, "I'm wondering how that was for you to hear." In essence, you are asking the other person to express what is going on with them having heard what you just shared. This is a critical piece of our dialogues that is often amiss. Most people don't ask this question because they fear the answer. They are scared the other person might be triggered and

—probably because of our own fight, flight, freeze response—we don't want to hear this. Unconsciously, we are trying to protect ourselves, so we don't go there. Unfortunately, this often backfires because the person is having their response anyway. Even if they don't say it aloud, they are thinking it. So, it's best to get it out on the table and unearth the need that is in play. In this way, we have more true safety, connection, and completion in our conflicts.

Without asking and hearing what is going on with the other, we leave a huge window for our default mode network to make up stories about the other person's experience and thinking. This is a place where our DMN can run amuck and draw from past trauma to make sense of the current situation, often misjudging what is actually occurring.

The back-and-forth use of all three Connecting Requests fosters greater understanding and connection and, ultimately, emotional safety for all.

Figure 18: Types of Connecting Requests

Request for:	Examples:
1. Dialogue	• Can we talk? • Are you open to talking about what happened, now or when you're ready? • Would you like to express yourself first?
2. Empathy	**Speaker asks listener to give empathy:** • I'm not sure I was clear. I'm wondering what you heard about my feelings and needs? • It's on me (not you) to be sure I communicated what I wanted you to hear. Would you be willing to tell me what you heard, specifically what I'm feeling and needing? **Listener gives empathy and asks speaker to respond:** • Did I get that right? • Did I understand your needs correctly?
3. Expression	**Speaker asks listener to express:** • How was that for you to hear? • After hearing what I shared, I'm curious what's going on for you? What are you feeling, what are you needing? **Listener asks to express:** • Thanks for sharing. Do you mind if I say a few words next? • I'd like to respond to what you just said. Would that be ok?

Please refer to Appendix B for a larger version.

Once connection is made, "I hear your needs, you get my needs," then we are ready to move to strategies to get those needs met. The Action Requests in NVC are the strategies. Remember from early on, we learned that needs are universal and what everyone wants; strategies are individual ways of getting those needs met. There is a placeholder for strategies in the NVC model. After all, all this connection around needs is lovely, but human beings really enjoy action: doing something regarding the conflict. The difference in the NVC model from how we usually do conflict is that most people, when in conflict, want to move to a strategy first thing. How do we fix this? What do you want the other person to do? In NVC, we make sure we understand the needs on hand first and then we move into strategy via Action Requests.

NVC Action Requests fit the following four criteria:

1. Positive: they are stated in the affirmative of what you want to happen, not what you don't want to happen. For example: "Be home by 8:00 p.m." instead of "Don't be home late."

2. Specific: they are given with as much observable detail as possible. For example, "Can you sit on the couch with me and watch TV from 8:00 until 10:00 tonight?" rather than "Can you give me some attention tonight?"

3. Present moment: they require an immediate commitment. For example, "Can you at this moment commit to brushing your teeth before 7:00 p.m. tonight?"

4. Do-able: they are something that the other person is capable of doing, such as exercise versus doing a backflip.

Before making an Action Request, however, remember to do a gut check. Are you holding onto an outcome? Will you be able to hear no and be okay with it? Part of making a true request is remembering that there are many different strategies to meet a need.

Another famous line of Marshall Rosenberg's is, "Hold needs tightly and strategies lightly." This becomes easier once we have taken the time to really get each other's needs. If you notice that internal grip around wanting a specific outcome, that is an indication there is some internal work to be done around your request. Deeply connecting to your needs via self-empathy (more on this later) and third-party empathy can be useful in lessening the grip and sourcing other strategies for contributing to the need underneath so that you can make the ask without the demand energy. And, like "dogging for your needs," you can ask it again and again—as long as the "grip" is absent.

WAIT

Figure 19: WAIT on the NVC Dance Floor

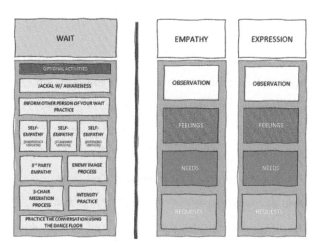

Please refer to Appendix B for a larger version.

So far, we have gone over the Empathy and Expression columns of the NVC Dance Floor, and we have reviewed each of their components. We have talked about how it is ideal to start with empathy first, use your Connecting Requests to cycle back and forth between hearing the other and sharing your own truth and, while doing so, using the Observation, Feelings, Needs, Requests (OFNR) training wheels. However, don't you find it rather difficult to really hear, without judgment, the other person in an argument? I still do, and I've been practicing NVC for a long time. When on the empathy line, we are striving for true listening, not just going through the motions of OFNR. If you find you are unable to hear the other, it is an indication that you, yourself, need some empathy. You likely will not get it from the other person in the conflict at the moment, so this is a huge indicator that you might step over to the WAIT part of the Dance Floor (Figure 19).

WAIT in NVC stands for "Why Am I Talking?" or "What Am I Thinking?" I love that WAIT stands for both questions because one points to the external part of the conversation you are attempting to have while the other makes you question your own internal process to take an honest look at the judgments in play. Both can eventually nudge you to separating out your judgments from your OFNR and give you a greater chance to connect with self and other. However, WAIT usually takes time *and* it occurs away from the other person in the conflict. Sometimes this "away" process is just in your mind as you are standing in front of the other and, ideally, it is done away from the other person physically so that you have ample time to process what is going on in terms of

OFNR for self and other. WAIT is not a cool-down period. You may cool down, yes, but WAIT in NVC is an active time in which you draw from several processes to help you expel demand energy, get clear on the feelings and needs in play, and get better prepared to have the conversation with greater success toward connection (individuals being seen, heard, and valued without judgment). As indicated, in Figure 19, some of the techniques you can employ during WAIT are:

- Jackaling with Awareness
- Informing other Person of Your WAIT Practice
- Self-Empathy: Emergency, Standard, or Extended
- Third-Party Empathy
- Enemy Image Process
- 3-Chair Mediation
- Intensity Practice
- Practicing the Conversation Using the Dance Floor

At The Bigbie Method, we offer practice sessions in our Empathy Gym, where people have a built-in, consistent mechanism for practicing their NVC skills, connecting with others, and working through these WAIT processes when necessary (www.thebigbie method.com). For now, the important takeaway is that WAIT is an active, conscious process. Sometimes, like with Emergency Self-Empathy, it can take a few seconds. Oftentimes, however, it takes some time; it may go on for hours, days, weeks, or even longer, but you are in an active process to become better connected with self and, ideally, other. You have full awareness that you are on this part of the Dance Floor and you are employing one or more of these procedures to separate out your judgments from the OFNR in play. Please note, there is nothing inherently wrong about judgment; we need it in many aspects of life to survive. But are we in conscious judgment or discernment, or is the judgment more about badness or wrongness—blame of self or other? In NVC, we call this jackaling.

JACKAL VERSUS GIRAFFE

If you've been around NVC at all, you have likely seen pictures of giraffes. That's because NVC is often referred to as giraffe language. This contrasts with another type of communication: jackal. The symbol of the giraffe was chosen because giraffes are quite tall and able to see long distances; they are also the land mammal with the largest heart. NVC is a heart-based language that requires extended vision. Jackals, on the other hand, are often seen as low-to-the-ground, predatory animals. Nothing wrong with our jackal friends; they just might not see the long view. In NVC, giraffe is symbolic of empathy, and jackaling represents blame or judgment. I like to point out that jackaling does not go away in NVC, because it's an integral part of the process. I love my jackal. It lets me know when a need is bound up inside of me trying to come to the light of day. The main difference in my jackal from before I learned NVC is that now I have awareness of it. It doesn't pop up unconsciously and jump out in my words. Instead, I have conscious awareness of my jackal thoughts, at least eventually when in WAIT, and I do my best not to state my jackal thoughts to the other in the conflict. I've found that jackal language does not help with connection. Back to the definition, once again, of connection being the ease and flow that occurs within and between people when they experience being seen, heard, and valued without judgment. Giraffe language or NVC empathy helps to create this, while jackaling is meant for one's own process, out of sight from the person with whom you are in conflict. In this way, all parties remain emotionally safe.

Now, if we return to the example I provided at the beginning of this chapter when someone said to me, "I am appalled by your vulgar language," let's see if we can break this down through the lens of the NVC Dance Floor and what we know about trauma response. Figure 20 shows my response. When I received the email, I got scared because of my fight, flight, freeze response. Remember from Chapter 2 all that has been programmed into me as a child and having a mother who would say non-observational things to me (judgments), often with a finger in my face, and in a tone and level that was hard for me. Receiving a judgment or jackal statement, especially when I didn't expect it, pushed my fear response. Many of us, in a moment like that, respond by either jackaling out at the other person (blaming them, saying things that they did wrong in an effort toward self-protection) or jackaling in at self, concentrating on what we did wrong and having judgments about self. Both jackal responses only continue the disconnection with self and/or other. Or we use some of those Other Conversational Responses, like explaining or minimizing or joking, and that often lead to disconnection as well.

FIGURE 20:
MY NVC PROCESS

When I received the email that contained among other things, "I'm appalled by your vulgar language," I did the following:

1. I stopped, breathed, connected to the sensation inside my body.

2. I labeled my experience with a feeling and a need. I felt scared and sad and the needs I had for myself were emotional safety, understanding, and kindness. The needs I mourned for him in the situation were sensitivity (from me) and emotional safety (for his young children who had heard my instructional video with the F word).

3. If I had any judgment about him, I kept going back and connecting with my sensations, feelings, and needs.

4. I wrote him back using only observational language and sharing the feelings and needs that surfaced. I ended with a request and an appreciation connected to my need for support, which he provided by giving me more strategies that I liked for the future.

5. I got empathy, after the fact, to keep from spiraling into judgment of self and others.

The alternative is to notice your response, your jackal thoughts, and/or your internal sensations and use both to begin to explore and connect to the needs underneath both. In so doing, one creates more clarity and less story-making about the situation. Then a greater capacity to speak to those needs, void of judgment and blame, results in greater safety and connection for all. The example of the email statement may seem "trivial," yet I believe we experience hundreds of these kinds of interactions daily. Many of them play out unconsciously and perpetuate the disconnection and then feed the passive violence which, in turn, creates the active violence we see in society. It all starts with awareness of our trauma response and our internal dialogue about self and other. And it can end with learning a new way of thinking and speaking that allows honesty and creates connection: enter NVC and The Bigbie Method.

The goal of this book is to interrupt the cycle of violence we see perpetuated in the world, everywhere. We experience this cycle in our homes, our schools, our businesses, and our organizations. Anywhere people interact, you can be sure this cycle is playing out, usually unconsciously. I am so fortunate that my work is my work. I get to use the NVC processes on myself and then share with others what seems effective in my own life. I have a vision of sharing what I've learned on a large scale because the need is grand. I'd like to contribute to millions of people and give them the ability/tools to create more love, peace, and connection in the world. At my company, called The Bigbie Method (TBM), we teach people how to create connection through communication, even in conflict. Next is an excerpt from my personal journal that I came across recently, where I am deeply committing this vision to myself and the world (Figure 21). The next chapter discusses TBM, how it came to be, and how it helps people in all segments of society to combat violence at the root level.

Figure 21: Writing from My Personal Journal on My Destiny Vision

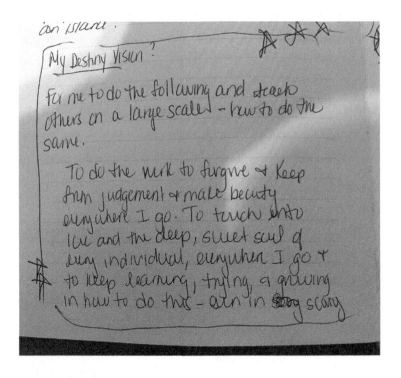

situations and/or when my own
fff is triggered. This won't be easy,
I will be challenged internally and
externally. It's my work to keep
working on this & to share what I
learn/experience with others

My destiny vision is to leave more (millions-maybe billions)
people w/ the ability/tools to create more
love, connection, peace + connection in the world

To be clear - I am far from perfect
with this - but I'm willing to be in
the game to be challenged and
do the work to live in integrity as best I
can w/ this vision. I realize I will
still have some disconnection - discomforts
w/ some individuals → and I probably
won't have time, energy, resources to
create connection in all these instances -
but when and where necessary - I will do
the work.

Writing from my personal journal on my destiny vision

CHAPTER 4

THE BIGBIE METHOD (TBM)

"Your work is to discover your work and then,
with all your heart, to give yourself to it."

−BUDDHA

OPERATIONALIZING PEACE!

This is the tagline for The Bigbie Method. It's a rather bold statement. Lord knows, we could all use a little more peace in our world. And given what you have read thus far, perhaps it makes a bit more sense why we see and experience disconnection and lack of peace in all corners of our world—in our homes, businesses, schools, organizations, politics. Underlying all of this, I believe that individuals' minds are working similarly to my own mind, which I share throughout this book. We make sense of our world based on our history and interpret situations through that lens, often from an unconscious activation of our fight, flight, freeze response. This is further exacerbated by our learned communication system, where we tend to mix up thoughts and feelings, use evaluations as if they are observations, instinctually jump into stating our thoughts without pause or the ability to connect with the needs in play for ourselves and rarely for others—all this feeds the frenzy. There is so much complexity in play.

When I have had the good fortune to participate in or observe interactions based in NVC, where those involved have had the ability and grace to slow down, get present, source the needs in play and set up a different quality of conversation, a window opens to what is really happening in our heads (thoughts) and hearts (feelings). Misperceptions and fears disappear, and connection and peace are created. I have great appreciation anytime I am involved in this miracle because it does seem like a miracle, given the stories and misconceptions that are surfaced (due to the individual's past trauma and what runs through their minds and bodies). I often find myself shaking my head, thinking, *It's amazing we get along at all.*

And yet, we can truly operationalize peace because peace relies on connection, and as shared previously, connection is not an abstract, touchy, feely concept. Connection is a concrete concept created by a set of processes that can be replicated and scaled up. Please recall Chapter 3. All the processes there lead to connection and thus provide more peace and have the potential to transform our individual and collective lives. And that is exactly the mission of The Bigbie Method. It doesn't matter if we focus on parents, lovers, friends, teachers, employees—the processes are the same.

It's been an interesting journey seeing the need for scaling up this model and trying, for years, to get that to happen. It requires integrity with the process at all levels. What does that mean? Growing this work requires me to walk the walk and talk the talk. I must work my own process as I interact with the world. When I have my own triggers and fears in my interactions as I teach the model or talk about it to "influencers," I must apply what I'm promoting. That can be quite tricky and difficult and amazing because promoting the work forces me to live it, struggle with it, and get better at it. Also, the critical component of NVC is presence, meeting people where they are, without force. This goes against so much of what we have learned in society, and it is quite a conundrum when one sees the huge impact of violence and trauma in our world and has an antidote for it, and the antidote itself is not forcing one's will. How do you get a movement to happen without force? Gandhi did so! And Nonviolent Communication, ironically (the name itself is often debated) was named as such in connection with Gandhi's work. But the name was given based on the idea that disconnection, in any way, is a form of violence. It was not given, as far as I know, to emulate the principles of the movement that Gandhi led.

So, I am left with this desperate drive to leave this work with as many people as possible, seeing its potential repeatedly and bound by the processes themselves to promote the work differently. As I play with the creative process of bringing this work to the masses and maintaining integrity with the process itself, I am fortified by consistent examples of "success," by which I mean shared stories of people in work, school, and personal situations where they used the process and created connection instead of its opposite.

I will share a few of these "success" stories shortly but want the reader to view them not so much as individually inspiring but more through the lens of compound interest or exponential impact. You see, each time someone shares their stories with me, I imagine keeping a tally sheet and putting one more mark down on the side of peace. These are little interactions, but we have hundreds of these interactions/communications each day, and each one can go north or south. Depending upon the direction of that interaction, our brains will lay down or reinforce tracks of trust or defense. This happens at the individual level, and individuals make up the collective. The point is that these little interactions matter immensely —if we can change them. When we can intentionally create connection in these small ways, and when we get the masses proficient in these skills, we will exponentially grow a concrete, palpable peace worldwide. At The Bigbie Method, we have developed a performance-based system that grows people's communication skills in the ways outlined throughout this book. If you are ready and dedicated to learning, we can teach you.

One thing I know for sure, individuals who commit to the NVC journey do have a greater sense of overall peace and connection in their individual lives. I pray I live long enough to see the compound effect of this work as it continues to grow in the world.

GOING NORTH INSTEAD OF SOUTH

In Schools

This interaction happened in a classroom environment with a middle school student diagnosed as Autistic. He came into the classroom upset because he liked a girl and couldn't figure out how to problem-solve around saying hello and couldn't focus on academics because of that. "It was all-consuming," he said later when he and the teacher discussed the interaction.

This student was, in short, displaying some work avoidance: not logging in to his educational platforms, not collecting his materials for the day, and throwing papers on the floor while mumbling angrily. He was also kind of fidgety.

The teacher verbally prompted him to get started a few times, but physically gave space because she knew that he was easily triggered when someone is too close for too long. Then she walked up to him to check in more personally, and that's when he said, gritting his teeth, "Would you please, politely, fuck off?!" The teacher responded, "Absolutely. I'm guessing that you're upset, and I'm picking up on how you might like some space?" (Note this is an NVC empathy response, taking Feelings and Needs Guesses.) He said, "No shit, Sherlock."

In telling this story, the teacher shares how she so badly wanted to correct him and respond immediately, but she didn't. She said, "I had to bite my lip and remind myself that 'winning that battle' wasn't worth it. I made myself go sit down and WAIT. I actually sat on my hands and counted. I checked in about fifteen minutes later (because the brain physically needed time to shift from an emotional response to a logical response for us both), and he was open to chit-chatting outside about what was up with him. I listened with 'giraffe ears,' then he asked for advice about how to talk to the girl he liked. He also apologized and said that he didn't have the mental space to do work and think about a girl."

For someone with Autism, navigating social situations can be easily overstimulating. He ultimately said that he just wanted the teacher to know that he needed space ASAP, which is why he used that tone. The teacher responded by asking that, in the future, he directly tell her that he's bothered (with or without details) so she can have a quicker understanding about how to support him. He agreed. This has been their way of working together ever since.

In reflecting on going north instead of south, the teacher says, "I still tell people to this day that I'm his favorite teacher because the other staff just get told to fuck off, not asked or asked politely. He has had fifteen incidents that were logged as significant, so the likelihood to escalate is there. Now he asks me for other advice and has moved on to liking a different girl."

In Business

This situation occurred in a large production company for natural gas-related equipment. The person involved, Stan, is the Coordinator of Production Optimization. He had been working for the company for a little over a year when this situation arose.

A crucial person in his department was leaving the company, and Stan was responsible for letting the person, taking over this other man's responsibilities, know exactly what they were. However, when the person vacated his position, there was a glitch in the company's communication system, and calls for this person were being rerouted to the sales department. The woman in the sales department, who was caught up in these calls and confusion, wrote an "upset" email to Stan and copied several others on it.

Stan went to see her to address the problem and greeted her by saying, "Hi. Are they still calling?" to determine if the issue was still happening. In recalling the interaction, Stan shared, "I came to see what the situation was, and then I got ten minutes of what I perceived as shouting."

However, thanks to his NVC skills, the situation did not go south. Instead of defending himself or providing explanations or any of the Other Conversational Responses, he seized his empathy skills. When she shared about this kind of thing happening two years ago, he recalled reflecting and taking needs guesses. When she directed blame at him—"You should know that the customers would be calling and upset"—he did not jackal back but instead leaned in with compassion and curiosity about the needs playing out. She talked in this way that was uncomfortable for him for close to ten minutes. Stan explained his reaction as miraculous. He had been coming to the TBM Empathy Gym for about a year and was waiting for an emotional moment when his NVC skills would come online automatically, and that's exactly what happened here. "There were moments when I was almost triggered, and then I was able to just stay with reflection and needs guesses, just like we learn and practice in Empathy Gym. And, as a result, I didn't take it personally."

Not only did Stan maintain equanimity throughout the interaction, but the outcome was surprisingly sweet.

First, he explained that by staying in empathy, he was able to get a real appreciation for this woman and her care and concern around the company thriving. "I saw huge energy around these needs for effectiveness and thriving, and it was so great to see that rather than having judgments about her." Also, there was some trust built between them. "She was expecting me to be upset back at her. I can see she gained trust with me because I didn't respond with anger and defensiveness." Stan also shared that prior to this interaction, he had little connection with the sales department, and now there is a much better connection with them all. He and this woman are on friendly terms, and he believes he could express with more openness going forward, if need be.

When asked how he would have handled this prior to learning NVC, Stan shared that he would have avoided the whole situation. He says, "I wouldn't have gone to see her. I would have responded via email and copied everyone, and I would have continued an internal dialogue of blame around her lack of control. I would have avoided her, and stories from others about how they don't contact her anymore would have just fed my story." Instead, he shared, "The same situation created connection because of NVC. I could see her commitment, and I gained more respect for her."

In Coaching

One day, Brett, who usually plays on the B team, was invited to practice with the A team so that the coaches could see him play.

On the field, one of the better players on the A team, Tay, was having a good run. He stole the ball, beat out some players while running and handling the ball, got all the way to the goal, and then missed the shot. Brett said, "We need to finish those"—to which Tay responded, "Shut up, you suck!" After practice, the coaches talked, in general terms, about players supporting one another, especially in their communications and in trying new things so that the team could grow. The team was told that, in the future, if their communication didn't promote emotional safety, it would be addressed.

Meanwhile, one of the coaches (trained in NVC) took Tay aside once practice and the team debriefing were over. "Hey Tay, can we take a minute to talk about that interaction with Brett?" With permission the coach proceeded (giving empathy first). "You know that team discussion was directed to you, but we wanted to keep you safe by not calling anyone out. I'm guessing in that moment with Brett, you were a bit pumped up because you made a really good play there, and I'm guessing you were also feeling a big mixture of frustration because you got it all the way there and didn't score?" He said, "Yeah, that's it." The coach continued, "When you heard what Brett said about finishing it, I'm thinking you were even more frustrated because you were already down on yourself. Is that how that whole interaction happened?" Tay admitted that's exactly what happened for him, and he apologized and said that he wouldn't do it again.

The coach then pivoted from giving Tay empathy and asked if he could talk about some of the things on his mind. He was then able to talk with Tay about emotionally safe space and leadership. "I told him he is one of the leaders and how much he affects the team. A leader wants to make everyone around them better. I asked him if he could hold himself to that standard. What was cool about this interaction was that I could literally see and feel Tay's energy shift once I didn't lay into him and just took empathy guesses. Since then, he seems to be much more focused on practice. I also know that small interaction laid the foundation for a strong and trusting relationship with him."

In sharing the story, the coach reflected on how most of the models of coaching he had experienced were based on yelling at players and the difference in outcomes connected to trust and effectiveness by going north instead of south.

In Life

Janelle was stuck at a stoplight and texting. The light turned green, and she was unaware of it. The man behind her laid on his horn and shouted, "Get off your fucking phone." While a bit frazzled by that, she became curious how it would be to move toward connection rather than speeding off and avoiding the guy. So, she intentionally set herself up to pull right up to the man at the next traffic light, opened her window, and had the following exchange with the man. "Umm…hello. Back there where you laid on your horn and said what you said, I'm guessing you were really frustrated and agitated and that you just really want there to be consideration and safety for everyone on the road? The guy was quite startled, not expecting this. He sputtered, "Um, yeah yeah…that was it. Sorry for that, for laying on my horn." The light changed and Janelle said, "Okay, have a nice day." And off she went...literally and figuratively north instead of south.

BLESSED ARE THE PEACEMAKERS

I love that last story best. It's a true story, and it cracks me up just imagining the interaction and the shock of the driver because this is not, typically, how our interactions go. Imagine the difference for both Janelle and the other driver. Can you see how the typical reaction of Janelle avoiding the guy at the next light, speeding away, or flicking him off models the fight, flight, freeze response and would create further stress and disconnection between herself and the other? What she did required her to use the executive function of the brain and step out of the fight, flight, freeze response. And, in so doing, she created a new world in just seconds.

Imagine the fallout of each of these stories if they had been handled in the "typical" way. In the school, the student would have likely been sent to the principal's office, maybe suspended, and further disenfranchised from his school and teacher. He certainly would not be learning academics or how to communicate and express his needs in a way to be heard. Have you ever heard of the School-to-Prison Pipeline? That is the phrase used for the research that shows the link between our school system and our prison system. Those suspended are the ones ending up behind bars. This teacher is learning how to break that cycle. Also, please note, the teacher was able to state what she needed. She had a voice and was heard as well. In fact, I would guess that there was more understanding and greater success in rerouting the student's behavior than in sending him to the office, which is the more typical protocol.

Same thing with the coach: he, eventually, got to be heard. And when he did speak (after first giving empathy), the player was able to hear him because the groundwork for emotional safety had been laid. And, lastly, reflecting upon that business interaction, I hear almost daily about workplace situations where people are miserable due to the moment-to-moment interactions that tend to breed distrust and disconnection. Imagine if everyone were skilled up like Stan; our workplace environments would more consistently celebrate productivity, trust, and connection.

Now imagine each of these stories multiplied by however many interactions we each have in a day in our workplaces, our schools, our homes. That is the goal of The Bigbie Method.

BIRTHING THE BIGBIE METHOD

My journey with teaching and spreading NVC did not stop at the Restorative Justice program. The work at the program was simultaneously exhilarating and tragic. Getting to know so many youths at such a deep level, creating a space where individuals from various segments of our community who otherwise would never know each other could learn to trust and love one another so deeply—the experience was spiritual, beyond our world, an honor, and a blessing. But, as time went on with the work, I felt stuck. I knew the potential and couldn't get the level of support while working for the city, in a governmental structure, to scale the work to the level necessary. Also, I was tired, deeply exhausted because of the secondary trauma I experienced by giving empathy to so many people suffering so much tragedy. I didn't even realize how tired I was until I went away to a nine-day NVC International Intensive Training (IIT) and received deep, extended empathy myself from some "very skilled and empathetic" NVC people. That was just months after one of the youths, whom I loved and considered a close friend, was shot one night after a fair and died days later from the bullet lodged in his throat. I was at Trent's bedside, watching the tear trickle down his face as he struggled to talk. I could see the love in his eyes and the sorrow that we had come to this. I watched in disbelief as his mother sang to God, with fist held high, as we laid him to rest. (There is a poem about this tragedy in Appendix A.)

The week after I returned from the IIT, something happened at work, and I decided on the spot, out of the blue, that it was time to leave the RJ program. That was in February 2020, weeks before the pandemic became our reality. Before I knew about COVID-19 and the great change that was about to occur, I decided that I would leave my coordinator position at the RJ program at the end of July before the new group of teens started. I made this decision suddenly with no forethought of what, specifically, was next for me. I knew it would have something to do with NVC because I was clear that this was my life's work, but I didn't know the form it would take.

I had a couple of significant things that occurred that ultimately birthed The Bigbie Method. One was that after months of planning,

I started a combined NVC training with teachers and students at the local alternative school. Because of recent shootings, this school had turned into a war zone. I had run a restorative circle there months before and given the youth voice around all the violence. The outcome of that circle was the request, by the students, to have "more of this." My combined teacher-student NVC training was the result of that initial circle. I was able to teach it for only one day because COVID-19 shut down our world one week later. But, in just that one session, I saw how I could take the model I had developed at the RJ program and bring it to schools. In doing so, I could train teachers how to be with youth in a different, power-sharing way, and I could give all the participants (adults and youth) NVC skills and knowledge. I could create real connection in a school community, and connection equates to safety—which every school in America is seeking.

The other significant thing that happened the week prior to the start of the pandemic was that I gave a presentation at a trauma conference. And, like always, people seemed very inspired and excited about my work. I say this because of the number of people approaching me afterward to talk with me, get more information, and share their contact information. I see this every time I share in a public domain about my work—lots of enthusiasm and interest. But I felt puzzled. On the way home, I called my sister and shared how I don't understand how all this enthusiasm occurs and then nothing happens to help me take this work to the next level. She suggested I talk with a good friend of hers who was a public relations/messaging person and who had helped some rather large businesses grow.

Enter Andrew Miller! After hearing about my work and my desire to get it to the masses—because we have a trauma epidemic on hand that is the catalyst for all the violence we see—Andrew gave me this insight. He said, "Your problem is you have been trying to scale this through a government entity or non-profits. To scale something, you must make it a for-profit business. And you need to call this The Bigbie Method." He explained that like McDonald's is to hamburgers, so shall be The Bigbie Method to NVC. I didn't really like the name; I feared it sounding egotistical and taking away from the NVC community already in place. When I tried to explain this to Andrew, he said, "I will help you no matter what because I think what you are doing is needed in our world, but I won't be nearly as excited about it if you don't call it The Bigbie Method." Thus, The Bigbie Method was birthed.

Birthed during the time of COVID-19. I never thought I could teach NVC in a virtual format and went kicking and screaming into it. I thought, *NVC has too much process work involved, too much connection involved. We can't do this virtually.* But working with my best friend from college, Denise Hale, who is a "talented" instructional designer, I was proved wrong. In fact, I think the instruction is better than when I taught it face-to-face, and now I can offer it to anyone anywhere in the world.

I've had so much support in growing TBM, but I'd like to mention two other key individuals for their contribution to the model. Ryan Bonhardt fell from the sky and has been helping me since 2021. He has built the entire backbone of our system and contributes in innumerable ways, but I think one of his greatest contributions was the idea of the TBM Empathy Gym. Dr. Jeremiah Murphy, a professor of astrophysics at Florida State University, who volunteered at our local RJ program and became smitten with my work has also contributed to the TBM model and vision. It was Jeremiah's idea to make the TBM model performance-based, which has allowed us to take "soft skills" and make them quantifiable. Yes, we can quantify connection and empathy.

Currently, The Bigbie Method has two components: the eight-week Introduction to NVC, which is delivered via self-paced content and Zoom sessions, and the Empathy Gym practice sessions in which students can enroll once they take the Intro training. The entire system is built to take what most people consider to be "soft skills" and to quantify them. This was another idea I resisted. My thinking was that NVC is about a consciousness, a way of being with one another. We can't put a badge system on that. It will take away from the sacredness of it. Again, I have been proven wrong. And, as I write this, I realize that the whole TBM system has been a work in progress, a creative process being shaped over time as we figure out the most effective way to bring the NVC human technology to the masses, the masses experiencing trauma and violence and who, in my humble opinion, desperately need a new way of being with one another.

Some readers might wonder how TBM is different than other forms of NVC instruction. The original model grew out of my work with the local RJ program and the unique arrangement of pairing students and teachers in empathy dyads where they would give and receive empathy during the NVC class, doing away with the usual power structure between adults and young people in schools.

This is still the ultimate vision for the school model. However, the big difference between typical NVC training and TBM is the performance-based level system that allows us to confirm attainment and implementation of skills. I am excited as I see individuals level up in our system because there is concrete evidence of them understanding and using the skills on a regular basis, which is the goal I want for as many people as possible in our world. The system itself is designed to create people living in integrity with NVC principles and processes and, once someone has leveled up, I have confidence that I can take them to the next step in facilitating learning for others. In this way, the system has a built-in process of growing capacity while maintaining integrity with the NVC process. Also, the performance-based system is set up so that people go through it as they are ready. This means that individuals can participate in the TBM Empathy Gym and choose to go through the level system or not. We want everyone to have emotional safety in the process; no one is forced to level up.

TBM was birthed in 2020, during the pandemic, with a focus on bringing the human technology into schools. My heart is with youth, likely due to my own trauma. I want all youth to have a sense of connection so that they can move with less fight, flight, freeze reactivity as they grow into adulthood. However, while TBM's initial focus was on schools, we knew all along that it would organically grow into other segments as well, and it has. Currently, TBM offers support to individuals, and we have the TBM Education Model and the TBM Business Model. If this book has inspired you, we would love for you to become a part of the TBM and NVC community.

Help us bring this work to scale. Help us take it into schools, businesses, and homes. To learn more or connect with us directly, you can visit www.thebigbiemethod.com.

MY #1 SUPPORTER

I didn't pay myself for the first two years of building TBM. In fact, I used my own savings to keep me and the business afloat. I was fortunate to be able to do that and fortunate that a few people saw the potential of this work in literally saving the world and offered me financial support. One of those people was my dear, sweet mother. She came to stay with me for a long stint during the pandemic and would quietly listen to me building this business from my office. She took joy in sitting in my living room and overhearing all my business conversations as I created the curriculum and format of TBM.

We took long walks in the morning, where I shared about the creative process and all the stars lining up for this work to come forth. We would both share about the awe of this effort and how it was literally birthed directly from the dark days of our family, our family history going back through time. It was not lost on either of us how the trauma we experienced through generations was being transformed into something that had the potential to reroute trauma for the masses. My mother understood, intimately, that my own "crazy," my own trauma passed through her, was the driving force behind my developing this work so that others, particularly youth, wouldn't have to suffer a childhood lacking connection (being seen, heard, and valued without judgment).

During these COVID-19 days, I could see my mother's own communication style beginning to change. As my number one fan, we joked about her being the only person who would listen to my podcast. I started my podcast, *All About Connection—NVC with Dr. B*, in the early days of TBM. And listen she did, with the unintended result of starting to have greater awareness of her lifelong, habitual thinking and communication patterns that had caused so much disconnection in her life. Our talks on those walks were the beginning of a lot of healing that took place between us, thankfully, before her passing. She was the most significant person I have ever lost in my life, yet I don't feel devastated by her loss. I have tremendous peace and completion and an integration of her being within me. I give NVC and mindfulness the credit for this. By building The Bigbie Method, it is my hope to give this level of peace and completion to the world.

I've wondered about the next chapter in this book and if it makes sense to include it. I'm glad I wrote it because it was definitely cathartic for me as I processed my mother's sudden death, and it also allowed me to capture these precious moments so they were not lost with time. However, I question the usefulness of it for external readers. My point in sharing it is to give you an inside line to the miracle of deep love and connection that occurred between my mother and me in our last months together and to share some of the serendipity that led me to writing this book. Neither she nor I were scared through our final physical moments together. I had more presence and joy with her than ever before. Yes, she was sick and, of course, one would think we would rise to a tremendous level of love because of that alone. But what I'm trying to convey by giving you the details of the last month's journey was how only love existed. Nothing else! And I credit that to our NVC work and that we had no mess to clean up in the end. I want that for the world! God/Spirit—call it what you will—wanted this love to be known and for people to understand the complexity behind the energy of the world and how it has the potential to move toward the good. It must move toward the good!

CHAPTER 5

HER DEATH

An Honest-to-God Rebirth

*"The day the Lord created hope was probably
the same day he created Spring."*

—BERNARD WILLIAMS

I came up with the name of this chapter one morning as I drove to the cemetery to do yoga with my mom. I'd been doing this graveside yoga every day since Mother's Day (two days after her passing.) It's profound and beautiful, a gift to be in communion with her and the world in this way. That morning, lying in bed, thinking about this chapter, I realized how much I wanted to get across how her ending was so perfect, it almost seemed like a sappy storybook ending. I was thinking about the dogwood tree across from her body, the symbol she clearly gave to me. And then, I looked up the meaning of the dogwood, and the Google god said dogwoods symbolize "love, faithfulness, and purity. Dogwoods are also seen throughout different cultures around the world as symbols for rebirth and hope, because they bloom every time spring starts." Is it a coincidence that the only healthy dogwood in Tallahassee is cohabitating with my mother? Is it a coincidence that I titled this chapter "An Honest-to-God Rebirth" before I knew what the dogwood represents? I will leave that for you to decide for yourself. It's not a coincidence to me.

My mother's ending was picture perfect. So perfect, it all seems more like a fairy tale than a real happening. It's a story to be told. Her ending was a story of love that I desperately want to remember. I want to recall every detail and hold it all as deeply as when I was living it. And as the days move forward and away from the month of her death, I notice this deep sadness because I want to live in that month forever, feel it alive in me for eternity.

I know that's not how most daughters think about their mother's death. And I hope here I can capture it, memorialize it, and help others understand. It seems significant. It seems like there is a hidden secret to it desperately trying to emerge. It is love or God trying to make itself known in a world, in a human mind, that can never fully grasp it. That's a mouthful, and maybe I'm just making much out of nothing, but I do think the story of her death is worth trying to tell.

OUR LAST FIGHT—A HEALING!

The saga of her demise, for me, started right about the beginning of April 2022. She died on May 5, 2022, roughly one month later.

But to tell this part of the story, we must first return to February 2022, when my mother and I had one of our biggest fights in years. Unbeknown to me at the time, it would also be the last argument we ever had.

I flew down to South Florida with the explicit intention of spending time with her and seeing her newly renovated condo. A month before I even got there, her trauma trigger was in high gear. She had, anxiously, talked with my daughter and my brother about where I was going to stay when I was there, how much time I was going to spend with her, making unconscious, kind demands on how it all needed to be. She wanted me to be with her and not stay at my brother's house or spend most of my time with him. This was never the plan but was very irritating to hear because it was the pattern, the dance we had always done. Her fear energy, her insatiable need to know that she mattered, that she was loved, worked to push people away because of the demand energy entwined with it. It was painful for me. I loved her, wanted and intended to be with her, but then had a bad taste in my mouth because it became forced upon me. I often teach in NVC if one has no choice in a situation, we tend to resist it, even if it's the most reasonable thing. That was my experience with my mother. I wanted to give and show her love but then became resistant because of how she demanded it. How sad, especially because I knew that demand energy was fully connected to her trauma, but I couldn't rise above it and access the love.

My whole time down there became troublesome and nerve-racking, wanting to make sure she was happy with how I was spending my time. There's lots more to the story, but I'm going to shorten it here so as not to lose my readers. The bottom line is it ended in a fallout. My mother pointedly said judgmental comments in front of a group of us. The words she used, dripping with sarcasm and an edge in her tone, seemed obviously directed toward me. "You EMPATHETIC, KIND people... can't even wait for your mother for breakfast. I would NEVER do that to my mother." Everyone was triggered but brushed it off. I was outraged. A lifetime of my mother's "fight" impulse, her instinctive reflex of labeling, describing others or situations in a way that didn't meet needs for safety, kindness, or effective communication came to a head.

When I asked her a few hours later if she was willing to hear how that affected me, she said yes. Here is where I went "wrong." When I teach NVC, I teach to start with empathy for other first. I didn't follow my own teachings. I was too triggered, and I thought she was in a place to hear. I was wrong. Instead of her hearing in the way I needed, she said she heard and then, in a familiar tone that I describe as sharp, proceeded to tell me what she wanted me to hear. I literally plugged my ears with my fingers. I turned into five-year-old Cindy, trying to protect myself and her from the onslaught of her words. It only made her shout louder. I tried to shout over her that I was not holding my ears out of disrespect. "I'm holding my ears because I love you, and if I hear what you are saying right now, it's going to cause more disconnection than connection. I'm doing this to protect our relationship." She kept shouting over me. I left. Went to my brother's for the day. I did sleep at her house that night, and we did go to lunch before I flew home, but it was all awkward and rather silent. That was my last visit with her. *Sigh!*

When I got back to Tallahassee, I regained my sanity, did my own self-work, followed my own template of how to move back into connection after disconnection—attempting, desperately and with difficulty, to live in integrity with the work of connection to which I have dedicated my life. I got empathy, did self-empathy, talked with my therapist, practiced being in the conversation. And then, I reached out to my mother to try again. Most of my family members thought I was wasting my time, that she could never hear in the way I wanted, but I knew, deeply, she could learn. And so, I attempted again over the phone.

This time I started with a little empathy, realizing that it must have been hard and scary to hear the things I said to her in that initial conversation—noting that she probably really needed safety and to know that she was loved. Given the childhood and lifetime trauma she experienced, it's easy to see from this vantage point how important it was to note and consider those needs prior to launching into what I wanted to be heard. From there, I asked to guide her in hearing me. I explained, with her permission, that telling someone "I hear you," but then pivoting into what you want to say does not give the person the experience of being heard. I directed her to reflecting what I was saying and listening for my needs. And I shared honestly and fully. She often told people how quiet and shy I was as a child and how she would encourage me to speak up and even shout if necessary. But, I pointed out, her own trauma response of labeling and judging people with her words, including me, was the very thing that scared me and shut me down. I remembered her calling me "selfish" with her finger in my face—and how, as a kid, I would just shut up and take it because it made the wrath end quicker, but how, in those moments, I hated her.

Miraculously, my mother was able to just listen. She slowly reflected what I shared, she took needs guesses, with my main need being safety. And she felt devastated and so sorrowful that her own daughter had a need for safety triggered by her behaviors. I know that saddened her at the core, especially given her own need for safety because of her own parents' behaviors. The cycle of trauma—handed down—one generation to the next. Until we learn and have the tools to stop it. That's exactly what that conversation symbolized for us: the beginning of the healing, the end of generational trauma. She shared her deep regret and my heart opened to her like never before.

At the end of my sharing, true to my NVC teachings, I asked her if she had anything that she wanted to be heard. And, again, another miracle… my mother said, "No, I think it's just important at this time that you be heard." I could have done backflips. Here was a moment I thought I might never experience.

Then, a couple days later, my mother called me. She said she was not sleeping well due to the conversation and my comment about "hating her." She had things she wanted to share. She wanted me to offer her some grace. We set up a time to talk, and on the day of our scheduled time, I shared that I was open and ready to hear her, but I was having a very stressful morning related to my work, and I wanted her to know I was not as resourced as I would like to be for the conversation, but I was willing to have it. She said, "Maybe we should wait," which was another glorious moment for me. My mother was gauging my ability to hear instead of, in her usual way, of forcing herself to be heard. Choir of angels singing…I made a point to set up a time to connect with her again so the conversation wouldn't linger. She was aware and appreciative of my intentional acts to have connection around this hard conversation and give her the opportunity to be fully heard. When I called her, she was too busy to have the conversation, and I told her to circle back with me when she had space. We never finished the conversation in person, but she finished it with me from heaven.

The day after we buried her, my husband serendipitously found three pages of notes she had written to prepare for what she wanted me to hear. I decided to wait until my visit to her grave on Mother's Day to read them. I was scared she would open a can of worms and I would not have the closure I desperately wanted with her. But, thankfully, when I read her notes right next to her, on that beautiful Mother's Day morning, there was nothing new there. It was the same story she had told her whole life—her trauma story, which she, sadly, never experienced being fully heard or known. And it was, this time, a request, not a demand, for me to write it and let it be heard by many.

OUR LAST MONTH!

My mother never aged. She didn't grow old the way normal people do. I didn't have any real sense of her being an old person in need of assistance or close to death. My brother, sister, and I had conversations as if that was some time in the future for which we needed to plan. It wasn't now!

At eighty, she was as vibrant and feisty as ever. Perhaps there was a subtle hint of time wearing its way, a slight hint of the cancer gnawing at her bones, but it was barely noticeable—just scarcely enough for us to put the thought, the realization of her being old, off to another day.

Hell, when the truth of her illness finally surfaced, she was still doing real estate closings from her ICU bed. True story!

She was a force. And that force, that energy lived fully right up until the end. And is still living fully through me, pouring out this story, these words, as I attempt to meditate next to her resting place. No resting for Marci, even in death.

Her end began in Pilates. How fitting! She thought she pulled something in her neck, reported being in severe pain. Couldn't get in with a doctor fast enough. Went to a chiropractor who cracked her neck and she, immediately, felt intense pain down her spine and ribs. She shared, over the phone, about this pain. She shared about not being able to get out of bed. I got her to come to Tallahassee so an orthopedic friend of mine could look at her neck.

That appointment was on Monday, April 4, 2022. He thought it was degenerative bone disease and ordered an MRI so that we could proceed with steroid injections to alleviate the pain. Though I knew nothing about what the next month would hold, I saw the first sign of my mother's true age that day. And, weirdly in hindsight, wrote this poem that day.

I am finally

Walking the plank
Like a sudden slap in the face
Except the sharp pain
Lives in my heart
A deep sadness
Settling into my bones
I thought she would outrace it
But death won't be fooled
By man's attempts
To cover it up
The wrinkles
The bruises
The deterioration
If you stay long enough
They will take over
Like a log left out in the weather
Trying to maintain its form
Why bother
Perhaps it makes the inevitable
That much harder to believe
One moment spring was here
And my heart was light
Taking in the sights and sounds
And then
In one second
Everything has changed

And I see clearly
Walking the plank
Spring is different now
Dreading the inevitable winter
And holding space
With this woman I love
Despite all the roller coaster rides
Despite all the historical trauma crazy-making moments
There is a profound
Devastating
Sweetness
In being able to care with deep tenderness
Wondering how I will balance all that god is handing me in this moment
Knowing everyone travels this same path and survives
That's hopeful
But the pain wakes me
In the night
May I at least learn how to sleep
As she learns how to die

Little did I know that two days later, April 6, she would have a stroke and I would have to argue with her to get her to the ER. That's when the end truly began.

THE HOSPITAL

Once at the ER, I saw, for a moment, my mother's dignity being swept away as the young nurses and doctors interacted with her as if she was just another old person with a stroke. They did not know she was a shaman, a healer herself. A force larger than life and able to heal life. She never had our respect regarding her connection to shamanism, but her death was proof of her deep relationship with this indigenous religion characterized by belief in an unseen world of gods and ancestral spirits responsive only to shamans. It was hard to take the shamanism thing seriously because it was juxtaposed by my mother, the Cadillac-driving, acrylic-nail-wearing, everything-in-its-perfect-place person. For those who watch the modern-day series *Grace and Frankie* (which my mother loved and watched, laughing hysterically from her hospital bed), my mother was the strange combination of Frankie and Grace. If I had to characterize her, I'd say she was a New York businesswoman, Jewish American Princess (JAP), diva, hippie, shaman, Bahai, badass. How is that for an interesting combination?

Whatever she was, she was inspiring in her last month. I held her hand as she was placed in the ambulance and was transported to the hospital from the ER. She looked dazed and frail, scared, but that didn't last long.

When the effects of the stroke appeared, the left side of her mouth was lopsided. She couldn't chew easily. Her speech was slurred. Her left hand was stiffened into what looked like a claw that would no longer work. We spoon-fed my once prideful mother, and the food fell out the droopy side of her mouth. She was unfazed. We painstakingly got her out of the hospital bed and walked her to the bathroom, holding her hand so she wouldn't fall. I thought she would crumble when she saw her face, but she was unfazed. When I held her up in the shower and cleaned her private areas, she was unfazed. All this tragedy became a dance between us. A dance of giving and receiving, a dance of acceptance, a dance of love.

BRAVERY AND LOVE

Instead of fighting what was, we turned to presence and fun. Because of my sister's ingenuity in figuring out what Mom could do to resume her functions, we played games like patty cake and played with play dough. And within days, the stroke effects disappeared. But Mom was not released from the hospital because, while figuring out the cause of the stroke, doctors found and drained two liters of fluid from outside her lungs and then wanted to find the answer to the question of what caused the fluid. She was unfazed.

While doctors investigated the source of the fluid, we turned her hospital room into a spa where she got massaged, foot-soaks with fresh calendula, and aroma therapy via essential oils sprinkled through the air conditioning unit. My daughter brought her guitar and serenaded her Ema. (Ema, which means mother, is what Marci's grandchildren called her.) We climbed into bed with her, watched and laughed at all kinds of TV shows and movies. Somewhere amid our fun, doctors found a mass in her lung; she was unfazed.

During these days in the hospital, my mom was encouraged to get up and go for walks. I have this clear image of my mom with the hospital gown engulfing her and those blue hospital socks with the grip on the bottom sagging around her feet, holding our hands as she walked down the halls, unfazed by her appearance in "public." I remember, with awe, how at one point she said, "Let's jog," and she tried running down the hallway. Again, we laughed. I remember how we begged the hospital staff to let us take her outside so she could breathe the delicious spring air. They wouldn't allow it because she was on a heart monitor. On her jaunt around the hospital, we stopped at the nurse station, and she informed them that she was "breaking out of here." She told them that she was putting her heart monitor on me, and it would sound really good for a while. On that same day, she became excited about the idea of having a birthday party for Mike, my husband, in her hospital room. His birthday was the next day, April 11. She asked us to bring balloons and enough pizza and cake to share with all the nurses and staff, and she started inviting all the hospital folks who entered her room.

We never had the party. Instead, that was a difficult day for all. She went for a biopsy. Her oxygen plummeted during the procedure. She couldn't breathe. She ended up in the ICU with a tube stuck in her back to drain the fluid that kept accumulating. Ultimately, the biopsy results confirmed the mass was cancer. She shrugged her shoulders, "Oh well." Basically, unfazed.

Days later, after we were moved to our third room, Dr. Wong, her pulmonologist, shared the news that the fluid they drained came back positive for cancer as well. She had Stage 4 lung cancer. I watched her reaction closely. She did hesitate. I saw a slight sadness in her energetic and physical response; it pierced my heart. But she recovered within seconds, ate her dinner right after the news, and then proceeded to make business calls. Unfazed!

The next day, I brought a speaker into her hospital room and, with loud music playing, my sister and I danced around the room. Mom laughed hysterically and swayed along with us from her bed. We all nearly peed our pants because of all the outrageous moves we were making. And, at one point, during our dance-off, my brother filmed and coaxed Mom into shouting, "Dr. Wong is *Wong!*" and, playfully, flicking him off. Again, we nearly peed our pants.

I do want to mention our evenings while at the hospital during those first nine days. To me, they seemed almost sacred. My mother insisted that we go home. We were exhausted and she knew it. But it was painful and scary to leave her when darkness fell. I wouldn't leave until she had received all her meds and we had gotten her to the bathroom to pee and help her wash her face and brush her teeth. We would put the bed alarm on because I knew my feisty, hard-headed mother would attempt to go to the bathroom on her own in the middle of the night, not wanting to bother or wait for the nursing staff. We would place this soft, black eye pillow over her eyes and put on her "crickets," from the Calm app, which soothed her. We would gather up the coolers and other stuff accumulated in her room from the day. I remember and still can feel the agony in my heart as I write this, tears trying to emerge, as I think about those moments. Standing in the dark after a day of pain and so much love. Not wanting to leave her. Worried for her well-being. Praying she would sleep and have peace. Prying myself from her. She was still my mother, taking care of me, insisting I go home and sleep so I could take care of her. I want to always remember the love and sadness and exhaustion I felt leaving her room late at night. I want to feel that grief in my heart forever; it holds me to her now. It confirms my love!

HEADING HOME – THE FIRST TIME!

We, finally, did break her free from the hospital. Once they took the horrid tube out of her back, we were able to take her home to my house. It was dusk. My mother was so frail as we moved her from the wheelchair into my sister's car. They followed me home and I, intentionally, drove them down a canopied backroad so my mother could see spring, all the beauty, the moss-dripping live oaks in the light that comes at the end of the day. We didn't know yet that her time was up for real. We were still waiting to hear from her oncologist. We were still waiting for our own ray of light as we took her home that evening. And we set up our own upscale, makeshift hospital room in my house, in my entertainment room—with her touchstones all around, a blanket she received on her seventy-fifth birthday with pictures of Mom and her kids and grandkids hung in eyesight from the hospital bed we rented.

A few days after we got her home, we painstakingly took her to see the oncologist. By then, she could barely walk. Dr. Paresh Patel gave us some hope. We learned all about cancer markers. Did you know they can now determine the exact genetic makeup of cancer cells and, depending on that makeup, known as markers, targeted treatments can be prescribed? Many of these treatments are very successful in abating the cancer, in returning some life to the cancer victim. Dr. Patel laid out the possibilities. If she had cancer "A," he said, "I guarantee she won't die of lung cancer." He said, "Fifteen percent of people end up with cancer A Markers." Then he proceeded to lay out the other treatment possibilities, given Markers B through G. He said without treatment or if the treatment didn't work, she had very little time left. Once the markers came back, he wanted to move fast to treatment. We left his office, holding on to a little hope and resumed waiting for days, days that seemed like years, to find out the fate of the markers.

Meanwhile, Mom was nurtured, entertained, and loved around the clock. The family took turns being with her. When awake, she was never alone. At night, we took shifts so that someone would be there if she had to go to the bathroom or if she needed her meds, or if she just needed some company. My brother, sister, and I, along with our spouses and my daughters, spent time with her and with one another around the clock. Now, looking back, I see the gift it all was. When was the last time I had four weeks with my brother and sister to hang, dance, laugh, cry, and even argue a little (due to the exhaustion and stress)?

BACK TO THE HOSPITAL

But her time at home was short-lived. Ultimately, we couldn't get her pain under control. We had to convince her that it was best to return to the hospital. We promised her we wouldn't leave her at all this time. We, sadly, packed her items and then called the ambulance to transport her back to the sterile, cold hospital. Lynda, my sister, accompanied her in the ambulance. They left at around 7:00 p.m. and she was, finally, settled into her new room at 4:00 in the morning.

I don't know how long the last hospital jaunt was. I believe I spent two sad, special nights there in between my brother and sister taking night shifts as well. So, maybe we were there for four or five days? Time became nonexistent at that point as days and nights morphed into one. Her pain was able to be controlled, thankfully, but she disappeared a little more each day, becoming weaker and less able to move. Getting her out of bed to go to the bathroom, in the makeshift toilet just two steps from her bed, was a herculean act. The wires going into her veins and glued to her chest were many, making it difficult to maneuver. She moaned and groaned from the pain she felt when she moved. It took two or three people to get her on the commode. Unable to pull down her panties herself, I would do it for her as we held her up and held the wires away from her body. She looked so small and fragile sitting on that commode, head down, shoulder slumped due to the pain. But, even in those moments, she joked and showered appreciation to the hospital staff helping. She was unfazed. When we finally resorted to putting Depends on my classy mother to keep her from wetting the bed, she was still unfazed and, to me, became more dignified than ever. Within weeks she had shed much of the earthly ego we all hold and was, in our last lived moments together, becoming more angelic, more like her true self, more just love. I've never had more presence, never experienced such an intensity of sadness, heartbreak, and concern that seemed overshadowed by love, acceptance, and pride.

Yes, I felt proud of my mother. With every person—nurse, assistant, doctor, social worker, case manager, pet therapist, technician (we had probably twenty different people each day who would come to her room for any number of reasons)—she struck up a conversation, smiled, poured out genuine compliments, and always gave a heartfelt thank-you, usually several times. It was weird how I wanted each person to know her, to know how this had all come on so suddenly. "Just three weeks ago, she was walking around just like you and me. She was doing Pilates, selling real estate. She had two closings from her ICU bed." I wanted others to be as awed by her as I, finally, was. I was awed by her spirit and its love of life and her acceptance that it was slipping away.

We have a hilarious video that I took early morning after spending a long night at the hospital with her. I think it could go viral if I put it out to the world. I think it's both funny and profound and captures her sweetness in those last weeks. Upon waking, I encouraged my mom to meditate with me, and we sat quietly in presence with our new day. Then, I laid out my yoga mat next to her hospital bed, told her I was going to do yoga, and suggested she watch and take it in. Rather, she joined me. As I moved, she moved as best she could... raising her arms around and around, lifting her legs, stretching. It was a sight... beautiful, and I could tell she was experiencing such pleasure, even from the simple movements. This lasted a good hour—us joined together in spiritual union, me from my mat and she from her bed. Anyone looking in on us might have thought the scene was kind of bizarre or funny, but it was sacred. The video she made near the end of our practice was her telling my brother to "Stretch it. Feel the life. Feel the cells. Do it every morning. For real. Stretch it. It's no joke. Feel the cells coming alive. Stretch it. I love you all so much."

Somewhere amid our new hospital existence, Dr. Patel showed up with the news. My sister, God bless her, was there alone when he came and, thankfully, Mom was sleeping. So, Lynda asked him to return the next day when we all could be there as he shared the devastating news: game over. The markers had come back, and the treatment that he could use, he didn't think was ethical to attempt, due to her weakened state. We moved quickly, called hospice, called the palliative doctor to figure out how to transition her pain meds so we could administer them, and got ready to return her home, one last time. When Dr. Patel returned the next day, my brother, sister, and I were by her side as he let her know he was out of cards. She was somber for roughly five minutes as the heaviness of our reality set in and then, mostly unfazed. We cried, but she seemed okay. I walked out of the room with Dr. Patel, asked the dreaded question, to which he responded, "Days to weeks."

It was a week.

HOMECOMING

And, still, that week seemed more like a sacred, somber celebration than an end to my mother's life. For weeks, my front lawn acted like a parking lot as people came and went, and in those last precious days, the "parking lot" filled up. I knew my neighbors had to be thinking, *What on earth is going on at the Bigbie's house?* In fact, one stopped her car and asked, when she caught me outside, "What kind of party is going on at your house?"—to which I shared the sad truth.

It was amazing to see how my mother diminished a little more each day. She was transported home by a company that my sister found, another one of her extraordinary moves, because the hospital's case management team said there was no ambulance to take Mom home, and we were scrambling for precious time at home with her. The nice guys who brought her to my house let her hang out on the front lawn for a few minutes on the stretcher so she could take in the sunset and breathe fresh air for the last time. Once inside, the round-the-clock vigil began. The massages, morning and evening meditations, bedside music, ice packs, laughing, crying, crawling into bed to watch *Grace and Frankie*, *Kim's Convenience*, and Obama's *Our Great National Parks*; this all went on around the clock. And she seemed to love every minute of it.

The hospice nurse came that first night. Tammy became part of our family and taught us things we didn't want to know, like the dreaded bed roll. This is how you set up the pads under the hospice patient so that you can move them. It would take two to three of us to move Mom side to side or up and down on her bed, as she became less physically capable. She may have been less able to move, sit up, eat, drink, even talk in the last couple of days, but her mind and spirit seemed more capable. It was hard to understand her words, which was heartbreaking, because I had a sense she wanted to say so much. Some of the precious words I could make out in her last few days were her marveling about the death process. She said a few times in a row, "perfect," and how awesome and beautiful this experience was and how grateful she was to us that we kept our word to keep her out of pain.

My brother had the night shift since he rarely sleeps, anyway. And he had one rather traumatic night with Mom, when she insisted on getting out of the bed, anxious she was going to defecate in it. He had no time to call us, just several feet away in the next room, as he helped her to the commode. He was on crutches due to recent foot surgery, and lifting her in and out of bed was nearly impossible. When he woke us to help reposition her because he barely got her back in the bed, he was clearly traumatized. Poor Steve! What he didn't know was the reason for Mom's anxiety and her quick rush to the toilet.

In the morning, Mom shared her "nightmare" with Len, her best friend who had flown from Ecuador to Tallahassee to be with her, and who happens to be a dream expert and was also my mother's therapist years back. Mom shared, through her barely remaining, whispered voice, that she had to poop and was terrified of the thought of soiling the bed and Steve having to clean it up. She kept saying, "It was a nightmare."

Len connected for her and for us all the real-life nightmare she experienced as a toddler, and why the evening's occurrence was terrifying for her. Somewhere around age one or two, Mom experienced her first psychic wound. I remember her sharing this story with me after some intense therapy when it resurfaced in her memory. She and her parents were on vacation at some Jewish resort-type place. It was still light out, and my mom wanted to be outside playing with the other children, but my Nana wanted her to go to bed. Mom didn't want to go to sleep, and Nana was frustrated. My mother's earliest memory is of being in her crib, all alone, crying, wanting to go outside to play, being stuck and at the mercy of the grown-ups around her. Then, her father came into the room and severely beat her and left her alone in her crib. Telling the story to me years later, my mother said she remembers going cold after the beating. I assume that was shock. All the vulnerability and fear of that one-year-old's experience was alive with her here at the end. Mom couldn't poop, was holding it back for fear and shame and exposure of her utter vulnerability. Here she was stuck in her adult crib, basically at the mercy of those around her, just like that little girl. Len told her, and we reiterated, that she could finally let herself be taken care of. She seemed to relax into that knowing but still held strong to her bowels until her final moment. More about that in a bit.

MY LAST MEMORIES

I have two last memories of my mother with a teeny bit of life left in her. Three days before she passed, my hairdresser, Ron, came and did her hair. What a chore and a delight! First, he spent close to two hours gently taking out the mats that had accumulated over the weeks of no showering. Please note my mother could barely move at this point and any movements were painful. Ron figured out how to wash my mother's hair with a washcloth as two of us held her head carefully so as not to trigger any neck pain. Mom literally moaned with delight as Ron held her head in his hands and massaged and cleaned her hair. In the end, he gave my mother back her dignity. She could die with the physical beauty she had maintained all her life. I was surprised by how much delight and peace of mind that gave me. After Ron left, my mother was desperately trying to ask me something—my ear right up to her mouth so I could try and make out what she was saying. Finally, I understood and couldn't believe what she was struggling to say. "How much do we owe him?" You see, my mother was appreciative and very lucid, even with all the drugs in her small body. True to form, mind intact, right up to the end.

This other memory is from right after Ron left, and the hospice spiritual counselor came to visit and recited the Sh'ma (the one I cited at the beginning of the book; my favorite Jewish prayer). Mom seemed deeply touched by the prayer, so I played, for her, the modern-day version of it in song. Again, Mom seemed to perk up. From there, I just started playing a bunch of Jewish music and then switched to the soundtrack of *Fiddler on the Roof*. It was super cute and intriguing how this music seemed to stir her, this music from her heritage. This music born into her cells. Mind you, my mother was not really talking or moving at this point. But, when I played the song "Tradition," my mother sat up, as best she could, and started snapping her fingers, and shrugging her shoulders, as is often done with this traditional, cultural music. It was adorable watching her do this and there was a reverence to it all. A reverence about her life, her ancestors, their country, and story. It was a testimony about a people and their life, their heritage, and a statement that they will always be relevant. It was a gift, and those of us present danced around her bed, singing and celebrating the moment with her.

That is the last remembrance I have, to which I will hold fast, of my mother's magnificent vitality, her spunk. That was Monday, and she passed on Thursday. But, even barely moving, drinking, speaking, breathing, her force was with us right to the end. I'm sure of it. She was aware and fully present to all going on around her. And her strong spirit would not let go, even with all the perfection of the process, even with all the closure she had, even with her in total acceptance of the transition. I chalk it up to the fact that she was just a badass. That tough, little body couldn't peel itself away easily. For three days, Tammy, the hospice nurse, kept saying, "I don't think she will be here by morning." And for three mornings, there she was, barely breathing but breathing still. We joked that she was going to hold the hospice record for holding on the longest.

On Wednesday night, May 4, Tammy said, "If I were to bet, I'd say she won't be here by 6:00 a.m." Mom was breathing about six breaths every minute. Steve, my brother, stayed on night duty with instructions to wake us if it seemed close. When I woke in the morning, Mom was still with us. I was relieved, thinking she would pass in the light of the day, which seemed so much more comforting than her going in the dark. At 7:30 a.m., I woke Lynda, my sister, because Mom's breathing was down to three every sixty seconds. We gathered at her bedside—me, Steve, Lynda, Mike, Marc—tears trickling. And we stayed there for about two hours when we realized she wasn't going anywhere, not yet. It remained like this the entire day. We had had so many anticlimactic moments when we were barely breathing, awaiting her last breath, and then, like the Energizer bunny...she just kept going. She went on like this the entire day; it was ridiculous. Those of us sitting in wait just started going about our business around the house, figuring this could last days or weeks. There was a lightness and even fun and jokes; in exhaustion, we lost a bit of the intense, moment-to-moment presence... "Did anyone check to see if Mom is dead yet?" That evening, I made margaritas for everyone, and it seemed more like a party hanging around her bed. I think Mom was holding on to see us have fun one last time.

Cinco De Mayo will never be the same. She died that night.

THE END

And it was somber and tender and sweet and devastating. Again, we were all there—me, Steve, Lynda, Mike, and Marc. We tracked every breath: two a minute, one a minute, one a minute, one a minute. We could see a little pulse in her neck, and then it was no more. Gone! Just like that. May 5, 2022, 9:36 p.m. My mother was here one minute and then, gone. To where? I find myself asking that question repeatedly now. "Where did she go?" I suppose this is what people mean by the mystery!

We had prepared for this moment. I saved rose petals throughout the week. We had those and candles and crystals sparkling around the room. We called the hospice nurse on duty, and she came quickly. Then, to the breathtaking music Lynda picked out earlier, she and I and the hospice nurse bathed my dear mama. We washed her face, body, and lifeless limbs. We combed her hair. And, yes, we cleaned the soiled pads under her where she had finally let go and trusted. Trusted that those around her would take care of her in a way that aligned with true love. We dressed her in a lacey white dress, quintessentially Marci. The final touch, lip liner and lipstick, and Lynda sprinkled rose petals all around her.

I lost it when the funeral home people came to get her many hours later. I wailed aloud and thought, *This is going to be bad. This is going to hurt deeply for a very long time.* I woke in the morning and continued my bawling. I was in extreme pain and turmoil about laying her to rest without ceremony, without something spiritual, grounding, meaningful. And then, like everything else, it turned out perfectly. With significant help from my community, we had a beautiful, soulful, graveside funeral service, complete with sweet rain and booming thunder at all the right moments. It was like Ema was speaking from beyond as we lowered her back into the earth. My sister and I wore similar outfits of my mom's bright clothes to the funeral. I know she was smiling from heaven, saying, "I told you so," meaning we looked good, and we should have done this a long time ago.

OUR LESSON IN LOVE

My mother had a perfect death in every way. She was eighty! She lived fully—driving, working, doing Pilates right up until she "pulled" her neck. That neck pain was the cancer that had spread. Her death journey was the perfect amount of time. We had a month to process the tragedy. We had a month of closeness, fun, laughter, and depth. We had a month in which day-by-day she diminished, lost her vanity, became more spiritual right in front of our eyes. We had a month to see her stiffen so that seeing her lifeless body at the end was digestible. She had a month in which she finally felt love. It was so obvious, so all surrounding, so demonstrative, so practical; she couldn't miss it—FINALLY!

Due to her trauma, my mother would sometimes share that she knew people loved her, but she couldn't feel it. During therapy, she tried psychedelics to help access wounds, old memories, places in need of healing, and I was told that it took her two to three times the normal dosage to get her in a visionary state where she could access those broken places. She was the epitome of fight, flight, freeze response. She learned that deeply as a child to survive. It kept her from the love that was there all along. And it kept us from fully receiving her love because it was oftentimes masked with her insatiable desire to feel the love she couldn't access. As her children, we were handed an enormous task of giving love freely and authentically to someone who had so much love but all the anger and insistence and mistrust that comes with being wounded at birth.

Thanks to Nonviolent Communication, my mother and I had several conversations in the past couple of years where we could talk honestly about all of this. For this I am very grateful. I am thankful for the painful argument we had just months before she died and the gift of healing and closure that she provided by hearing me fully finally. And then, we got to top that off with a month of pure love. I've never enjoyed my time with my mother as much as that last devastating, beautiful, tender month.

Now, in the wake of my mother's death. I don't feel devastated. I miss her some, but I'm not in deep pain. If I'm in emotional pain at all, it's because I have judgment on myself. The old "you are selfish" with a finger in my face is attempting to awaken. How can I feel so good? How can I feel such peace? My mother is lying ten feet under the ground across town. I'm grateful to notice this is my childhood wound trying to wreak havoc. I'm grateful to connect the dots and call my therapist. I'm grateful for NVC to help me put reality in observational terms and deeply greet and sit with the needs I have, the ones I am celebrating and the ones I am mourning. It is a true gift to know how to process this and use my wounds to develop greater compassion for myself, and ultimately others, instead of perpetuating the trauma, which is what most of humanity does. This doesn't mean that I am perfect with it, like there is some nirvana that I get to reach eventually. But, perhaps, the peace I feel around Mom's death has a lot to do with the work both she and I have done over years to process our trauma differently. I say "perhaps" because the "selfish" demon is still there, keeping me from my perfect peace. There seems to always be work to do, but the demon is quieter, weaker, the peace stronger, more certain.

In NVC, we learn to see things through the lens of Observations, Feelings, and Needs. In the end, my love was so real, so strong. There was so much deep care. Everything else became secondary. I loved this. I could see the beauty in all of it; I experienced the opposite of selfishness in me. I was not resentful of spending all of spring in the hospital. I looked forward to it. It was a mission in a way. Waking up, hurriedly packing up for the day in the hospital, making her hot cereal or a smoothie, walking in, seeing her, and feeling happy, and she was happy too. Feeding her, talking to her; it was all so pleasurable. And she was so grateful, smiling, laughing, expressing her love and acceptance of it all. It was fun! We were complete. And while I am mourning a need for acceptance of my acceptance, I am working on receiving the peace that she would want for me. This is the gift of being able to see things through the lens of Observations, Feelings, and Needs, the gift of social intelligence. We learn how to process the world's stuff with a lot more clarity and a lot less blame and harm to self and others. If we all had more of this intelligence and these skills, we would have a greater chance of interrupting generational trauma and the violence that gets handed down, often unconsciously.

And this is the choice we, as humanity, get to make. Do we begin to teach emotional intelligence, how to know and process emotions, how to communicate cleanly without judgment and without perpetuating harm on self and others? Seems like this is foundational and probably as important as the fundamentals that we typically teach in school. As I write this, the nation is once again processing the news of a mass shooting. This time in Uvalde, Texas. This time twenty-one people died, nineteen children. I have thoughts of my mother holding and comforting each of these children somewhere in heaven. She was good at that. She was able to nurture, love, and ease pain in a way that she never received. I hope she holds and comforts Salvador Ramos too. He is the one that many will hate or fear or resent. I wonder about the story of his historical trauma. Where were things left unsaid or unprocessed? When I think of him, I notice a tension in my shoulders and something around my heart keeping me from breathing fully. Fear? He is the one that the world will have thoughts and judgments surrounding. He is the one that will stimulate the fight, flight, freeze response for millions and millions who will not know how to process all of this productively and keep the anger and resentment going. This is what we miss by not teaching emotional intelligence and NVC in schools.

I spent my last night in the hospital on April 27, sleeping on the quasi-pullout chair. I left the hospital around 6:30 a.m., just as the world was waking. Sitting in my car, I searched Spotify for a poignant song to accompany me on my ride home. I wanted to hear something beautiful, something meaningful and significant as I drove down one of my favorite canopy roads, watching the morning light break through the live oak trees. It had been merely hours since I had learned that my mother would die in "days to weeks." I wanted to feel that moment deep in my soul. I know music has a way to help one feel deeply; I needed something special for this final ride home from the hospital. And then, the Adele song

"All I Ask" serendipitously came on my car stereo. My immediate reaction was to change the song. "I don't want to hear this right now. I need something meaningful." But I decided to listen; I had a strange hunch even before I took in the words, that maybe this song was given to me, a gift.

It was like I was in a scene of some movie. Driving down the canopy road at dawn, I played the song over and over. Crying deeply. Hitting my hands on the steering wheel. Shouting "Oh my God, Oh my God!" Not out of sadness but out of amazement, out of awe, out of beauty and love. Love beyond all explanations.

Here is a link to the words of the song with Adele singing it: https://www.youtube.com/watch?v=rRWJcxa6mdo. Unfortunately, I have been advised not to print the lyrics here due to copyright laws, but if you really want to glimpse the miracle and strange "coincidence" of that song playing right in that moment, please take the time to listen to it. I think it will provide you with the final note to this story. It was meant as a love song between a couple, but if you listen, just think of the context in which it played for me. Pull out your phone and listen to it now if you can. Every word of it is significant, however, two lines leave me shaking my head, breathless, heartbroken and heart open: the ones about love's lesson and remembering us.

They seem to wrap up, with a perfect bow, my life's journey with my mother. The trauma passed down through generations, the way it played out between us, the love she gave that she wanted as a child, her inability to feel love, and the unconscious demands and judgments placed on those she loved to fill that void. Thankfully, the journey also included my work with NVC, learning how to break the cycle of the blame game, learning how to have authentic, difficult communications, processing hurt, and truly forgiving. Interrupting the cycle of trauma.

I am so grateful that, in my last month with my mother, I was finally able to hold her physically, emotionally, and spiritually with deep love and admiration. This journey, and we both knew it, was also about sharing our story. Part of our recovering connection in her last couple of years was her amazement at my work with The Bigbie Method. She knew that it grew directly out of history, our pain, and she also knew the potential it has for turning generations of trauma into healing and a new way of using conflict to create connection instead of devastation. Our story is your story. It's humanity's story. It is an example of love's triumph. It is not an end but a beginning, like the dogwood tree by her grave. It's a sign of rebirth and hope in an ongoing and never-ending journey of being imperfectly human while bound to our bodies. I love you Mommy, so deeply. I pray I did justice to your story. I pray I made it meaningful and useful for many. I pray you feel, deeply, my love for you up in heaven and forever in my heart!

Appendix A

Much of my writing comes in the early morning. This entire book fell out of me. I knew I would always write it, but when my mother asked me to do so on her dying bed, years of thinking about this work was catalyzed into existence. There was very little effort. My being would wake early, usually between 4:00 and 5:00, and I would essentially sleepwalk into my office and begin writing. It was easy and very pleasurable to create. I did try, one time, to write in the middle of my waking day, but it was a very different and strenuous experience. So, I have honored the life force waking me and coming through me. I've heard that we have greater access to spirit in those moments between sleep and wake because our subconscious is more accessible. This has been my experience.

What follows is a compilation of some of my poetry. I numbered them for easy reference. The first five, I think, explain themselves; they are poems that poured from me in the last month of my mother's life as I processed, tried to capture, and hold onto the depth of all the pain, the learnings, the love, and the beauty.

The sixth poem is the one I put on her gravesite on Mother's Day. She asked me to give her that poem for Mother's Day several months prior and before I knew she wouldn't be there physically to receive it. It felt smooth and seemed fitting with the flow of these writings to put it there in the sequence.

The remaining poems are ones that also dropped out of me, organically and cathartically, during my time working with youth.

Working at the local Restorative Justice program was the most eye-opening, heart-opening, and heart-breaking experience of my life. From 2012 to 2020, when the pandemic hit, I shaped a nationally recognized program that integrated the work of NVC and Restorative Justice. We served youth, ages thirteen to seventeen, most of whom were referred to us due to their involvement with the legal system.

Each youth in the program was required to participate in a restorative circle at the beginning and end of the program. Those circles were composed of the youth, at least one member of their family, the program staff, and three to five community members. This is where we got to know one another and figure out how to best serve the youth. There was a lot of magic in the process because we approached the entire thing through an NVC framework of honoring and keeping everyone emotionally safe and held—even though the youths were there because they "broke the law."

Throughout my time there, I would often dream of everyone in the white, middle- to upper-class world sitting in those restorative circles with me. I dreamt of this because I believe that we would have so much more support, sensitivity, and insight into poverty and race issues as a result, and I know (from experience) that the walls that separate us from one another would come down. It was the greatest gift to know my clients and their families. I want you to know them too. Bryan Stevenson, the hero attorney who wrote *Just Mercy* and who is known for his work of freeing innocent men from death row, talks passionately about the importance of proximity—how we need to get close to the situation, close to the people. This closeness drives deep understanding, connection, and, consequently, actions.

The poems from number seven on, I hope, provide a window into my experience at the program and into the souls of my friends, the teens. These pieces are shared with the intention of giving you some proximity. The names and specifics are changed to protect the youth. I wrote them as I lay in bed, usually having a hard time sleeping, because "my kids" weighed heavily on my mind. I'd grab my phone, open the Notes app, and let the words organically empty out of me. They were never intended for an audience. They were a way for me to process and heal the trauma I witnessed daily and to capture and celebrate the brilliance, resilience, and amazing spirit of these kids. The joy and devastation I experienced knowing them was more intense than anything I've experienced in my life. In sharing these writings here, I hope to give you a visceral, felt understanding of them and the experience of crossing the divide between black and white, young and old, poor and well kept. I hope to give you an inside view of the deep trauma so many of our youth experience daily. And I hope to inspire you to contribute in whatever way you can to help break the cycle of trauma.

1. Some Things I've Learned

In the past few weeks
How to do a bed roll
When your loved one is too weak
To move herself
The level of oxygen
One needs before calling 911
Signs of a stroke
And how the droopy mouth and limp stiff hand
May not be permanent
How the hospital lacks
The basics
Food Air Sleep
And how there truly
Are heroes in the medical field
Cancer markers
Tumors in organs
Can't be felt
But
Tumors on the bone
Are
Excruciating
Where my local cancer institute is
How great and connected and sweet my family is
How much my community cares
And
How deeply and intimately

I love her
Despite her handed-down trauma
Despite her faults
Love has risen and remains
Amen

2. How to Explain

The deep sweetness
I experienced
Sadness
As I washed away your vanity
And you let me
With a strong acceptance
And small frail bruised body
I shampooed your hair
Washed your ass
As you barely hung on
To the silver rail
With hands no longer able to grasp
But with a soul that can
A courageous heart
Surprising me
And humbling me
As I bow to our lives
And your awe-inspiring willingness
To embrace your
Drooping face—
Drool and all
Entering a new form of beauty and joy
As you let go of all you have clung to
Going down the drain
With the swirling suds

3. The Last Three Tissues

In the box
A sign of the finality
Finally
As her small framed
Goliath spirit
Breathed
Her final shallow
Hallelujah
Peaceful
Breaths
After a lifetime
And
Nighttime of fighting
And honoring the life
Within
Sitting patiently by her side
Oxygen machine
Pulsing slowly along
Like her heart
Waiting with our own heavy hearts for the end to both
But you have left us with
Lessons and love and
Cricket sounds with a new meaning
Just like this day

4. I Liked

How everything stopped
And we attended to
What needed tending

Like listening for hours
To her breath
All together
Holding hands
Singing
Waiting

Breath
After
Breath
After
Breath

And then
The oxygen machine
We unplugged

And hesitantly
Plugged back into
The life we left

Changed forever

5. Life

Has a way of stiffening us up
Most mornings we wake
And ache as we age

But to live the life
We must learn to lean in
Move stretch
Face the pain
Head on
Breathe
Even when it hurts
Even when we are tired

Staying present

Life is calling
Until the end
When the soul says enough
When it's no longer
Entwined with our human being
And the being part separates
Ashes to ashes
Returns to the soil
Metamorphosizes

Breaks down
And
Becomes the very thing
The essence
Feeding all of life

So why stiffen?
It never ends
You truly are the source
All is well
Don't be tricked by form
All is love!
Live your life
All what is given!

6. Waking in Darkness

I walk to my space
Light candle
Assume seat
Reaching desperately
For you
In the dark
Busy wandering mind
And then
It's there
The morning call
So subtle yet strong
Don't miss it
My own personal song
That bird
Her strong clear notes
Profound sound
Juxtaposed
Against the quiet morning
Mostly absolute silence
Except for the dull morning hum
Of cars barely heard
Taking people to the busyness of their day
And my bird's friends
Waking in other parts of the neighborhood
Their songs lightly heard in the backdrop
An offering to my fellow men

To wake up
Pay attention
Beauty is right here
If we only note it
I wait in the darkness
For the sound of life
Calling for me
So loud
So profound
Through my feathered friend
Whom I never see
Never recognize
But who sings to me
Every day
Just like you dear lord
Waiting for me to wake up
And recognize your call
Begin my life
Everyday
With you
Tucked away
A melody
Deeply entwined
In my soul
Waiting for me to know you always

7. I Live in Two Worlds

Every day
I'm blessed to work out north side OTF
Drop $150 each month
And shit in the bathroom
Supplied w Q-tips, deodorant, hairspray
To start my day
Toilet bowl sparkling clean
I love it
And the people so kind, considerate
Wrapped in their perfect bodies
And relatively petty problems
I wish they could slip into my skin
Occupy my brain

Occupy my other world
At least for a week
At least for one or two circles
To know the people
Of my other world—
South side

Instead they sip their morning coffee
Read the morning paper
And their minds
Get stamped
Everyday

With the morning mugshots
Of black men
Men/boys
Guilty before proven innocent

Over and over
That black image stamped into the white man's heart
Enough to make them turn away from the black souls
Waiting to catch the bus
Riding their bikes
Walking walking walking across town
Enough to keep them
From being
Up close to south side
It's a dangerous place
Full of dangerous people

Won't let their children cross too much
Over the border
Not worth the risk
Even with their modern-day
Open minds
Yes, we embrace diversity
But from afar
And only by barely touching our
Pointer fingers
Rarely really an embrace

After sweating my frustration and awareness out
My morning ritual

I shower off the perfection and cleanliness
And
Then
Step
Into
South side

Where the roaches wait for me
Run across my desk
And I shit in the bathroom
Supplied with toilet paper
Sometimes
But not on the roll
Toilet bowl with scum around the ring
Even on graduation day
That's how much we value our kids
How much we need to keep
The public trust
Paper towels cost
Too much

And I'm grateful to the public
To be here
To do this work
And know south side
Much more than
A mugshot in the morning paper

I'm grateful for the awareness
The awakening
To look for my friends
My family members at the bus stop
Riding their bikes
Walking walking walking across town
I understand now
I see way past that separating image
Image
Image
Daily stamped image

That at one time made me afraid
And not see the person
The people
The beauty of this land
And shut me off to the truth of how
Blindness
To our history
To the lynchings perpetuates the problem

It's so much easier
To look at mugshots
Cast judgment and pity
And continue running on my treadmill
Instead of walking walking walking across town
And giving a handshake
A true embrace

I long
Deep in my heart
I carry pain
For the morning
Of shared understanding
Awareness
And so much support
So much northside goodness
That I don't experience my morning bathroom business so differently

And we are all truly one
Amen

*OTF = Orange Theory Fitness

8. Sorry to Disturb Your Sweet Slumber

But there is a debt
A healing owed
And it requires you to wake up
Humanity's soul is broken into a million pieces—
All hands-on deck to set the cast

I know
I know
It's so cozy in your innocence
So cozy in that blind slumber
With your down comforter and 900 thread count sheets

But ⅔'s of life is daytime
With its rising sun—brilliance—ray of light—
hope streaming through the glass

Go out in it—rejoice and beware
You may also drown in despair
There's enormous beauty and also violence out there

Wake up
Peel yourself from comfort
It's okay to sacrifice—at least something
Perhaps a repurposed gift or
At least your attention

Hear them

See them

It's meant to be bothersome

It's meant to stir something in your soul

It's meant to make you get off your ass and contribute to the

point that you are a little inconvenienced

In fact—this world depends on it

Life depends on it

I've seen their suffering

And their soul resilience

God gave it to everyone

You have enough strength to do without your cozy bed

Embrace all of life

Reach out your hand

Get up close to something that breaks your heart

There will be a gift waiting for us all there

Far better than that heating blanket—

which keeps you from touching the cold

Awakened floor

Proximity gives

A return on investment—

Up close and personal

The gift is

Connection

And the ability to lay down your head

To rest without your noise machine and void of your

Ambien lulling you into slumber

9. Warren

Can't possibly be the same kid
Who cursed out Vang
the Language Arts teacher
You fat mother fucking bitch...

He can't possibly be the same kid
Who pounded his fists into John
The ex-navy dude
Now turned super teacher
Who for the very first time
ALMOST lost control
With an avalanche of obscenities
Accompanying the hate-filled spit
That landed, splat, on his face
This gentle strong spirit
Was almost driven to joining the insanity

He can't possibly be the same kid
Who bit the massive man asst principal
All 330 pounds of football muscle
Struggling to restrain the little boy
So filled with rage from years and years
Of yelling and homelessness and hunger

Poverty is disguised in so many ways
Often with slick sneakers and an energy

Of violence begging for someone
to figure out the puzzle—
Even if only his own broken soul
Someone make sense of this monster

He can't possibly be the same kid
Sitting in Tuesday circle
Leaning in
Listening for some clues
To his own craziness
As we teach about
The effects of trauma
On the brain

He can't possibly be the same kid
Sitting in the Tuesday circle
Saying
Out of nowhere
I used to not like this class
But I kinda like it now...
A little

Blessed to unlock the secret
Connection First
Absolute no judgment
We are gonna hold you
Sacredly safe
We are gonna hold your hand
And your heart so gently and strongly
And guide you to another world

A world where kids are fed
And grown-ups know how to speak
Without the blame and judgment
That only feeds the violent flames
Of trauma

He can't be the same kid
Or can he?
You choose
Love or hate
What will we perpetuate?

10. Jasmine

Metaphorically
We'll wear that blood-
Soaked shirt forever
That blood-soaked shirt
She wore for three days
After Joaquin was shot and killed
Right after their fun night
At the game

I saw the video
Posted
Two bodies down
Lights flashing
Police assuming the role of medics
God bless them
Trying to keep the life from leaving
Jasmine—all of four foot eight?
Watching
Hands stretched upright—shaking
Like an offering
A prayer
Keeping the blood from dripping deeper into her being
Watching as her loved one slipped
Away

Before that night I never saw them apart
On that night
I heard she held him in her arms
As he bled out
From the hole in his head

And I know her
She has endured a loving daddy who
Can't help but drop the f bomb and more at her
At a very young age—
Along with his genuine love and concern
She has endured a loving mom who also has endured tragedy
And, I think, copes by checking out on drugs

Jasmine's stability was Joaquin
She wore his blood for three full days
Refusing to let go of the best love she has known

And
Like it or not
That blood-drenched garment
Is an extension
Of her own skin now

She wore that shirt for three days
To make sure
He would always be a part of her
For good or for bad
Together forever

11. Jontavion

I found him
In a thing
A thing acting as a house
Down a dirt road
In Bradfordville.

Dear God. Surely no one lives here—please don't let this
rusted tin can, barely standing, be his home.

He breathes relief as we sit in my makeshift office—car. So cool in here.
It's hot hell in that blue box home.

I've come to seek him out.
To make connection—in exchange for presence in my class.
And, once again,
I'm rewarded with the person.

Jontavion. Scared to be at the Center.
He's north side.
Too many south side kids there.
Jontavion has to keep constant vigil.
Look over his shoulder—ears perked up
Like a deer in hunting season.

Jontavion whose mother is a "crazy bitch"
Whose older cousin, by one year,
Stabbed the crazy bitch and now

Gone for 45 years.

Younger bro—he's gone too.
Jontavion—His Sissy—
Calls the police on him when their fight gets too big—
The fight started because he won't sell drugs for her.

Jontavion who first came to us with marijuana pouring out of his organs.
Weed the salve
For his abandoned soul.
The soul I see clearly—locking eyes.
So much love and want for love. So much longing—
Is trust a real thing—
Wanting to believe so badly.

So deep in the woods.
So deep in despair—
and yet in his essence—I feel love—
and I'm honored to touch that depth.
And I pray for his resurrection out of the mobile home—
on that potholed dirt road
in Bradfordville.

12. Cal Stutz

He shot his sister
By accident
Mom had to bury Zannie
Visit son behind bars
And move from section 8 housing
(No violent crimes allowed)
All in one week's time

Gun bought
"To protect family"
And those across town roll their eyes
Casting judgment
How silly
How stupid to have a gun
Really?
Have you walked south side?
Waited for the bus by Joe Louis Street?
Heard gunshots constantly?
Seen friends and family taken out?

I roll my eyes at the concealed weapon
Gun-carrying-permitted white dude
All those Walmart customers with guns on their hips
What are you protecting with your righteous weapons?

Cal had a gun
Shame on him
Playing with his siblings
Like I see them do
Horsing around
Loading it
Unloading it
Pointing it

Zannie—lying in her bed
"I'm not scared of you. Lol."
Bang!!!!!!
Dead
Gone

The funeral
Cal—front row,
Next to mom
Open casket
Sister laid out

DJJ allowed some closure
But he paid with
The walk of shame
Handcuffed
Legs shackled
Head down
Down the aisle
Teary-eyed mourners
Shaking their heads

Watching him walk
Right before her casket is rolled out

How does one go on?
How does one make a new living?
With the four remaining siblings—
In the "new" home?
Cockroaches from the past moved right in with them
Crawling over their stained mattresses and out of
the cracks of the dresser mirror?

How does anyone start anew when plagued with poverty and the violence/
protection that erupts out of desperation?
-

I don't know the answers
I just know not to roll my eyes at them
It's complicated

13. Justin

Rickards football stud
Loved by everyone
Tells me how
In 8th grade
The high school football coach
Marched a group of them
To see the billboard on south Monroe
Flashing that year's
Rickards High school
Football seniors
Leaders of the team
With bright futures ahead

But not Justin
Not this boy
With his slow steady smile
With his way of greeting the secretaries at the front desk
He was everyone's son
Just had that way about him
That made you love him

Once again
Trauma rules
Did anyone know of his mother's debilitating illness
That rendered her beautiful

Brilliant self
Unemployed—
Barely able to walk?

Now his brother—
One year his elder and best friend—
Sentenced for a long time
Justin was there as the prosecutor painted a picture of his sibling
As a monster Justin did not know
He shared w me through tears and a clenched fist

Justin barely squeaked by a similar fate
The day his brother was arrested—
He too was taken into custody
Arrested
And eventually charged with a felony

Brother had burglarized some homes
Making ends meet
Hid his gun in the bottom of Justin's backpack unbeknown

Police raided the home
And when mom couldn't leave
Police offered to pick Justin up at the park
He was searched before entering the vehicle
Gun found
Life forever changed

The principal cries
The day he expelled him
District rules
No felonies allowed
No football
No billboard
No college scholarships

That backpack and gun
Followed him
Carved out a new path
A much harder
Uphill climb
With a baby on his back
At twenty
And night shift at Lowes

Still life goes on
Life goes on
I sit with him and mom and baby's mama
Visiting 14-day-old beauty
And I don't feel the joy
Only exhaustion
Barely anyone talks
Is this the new baby
Or just life with its heavy weight
Keeping them from rising
And laughing with joy?

I don't know
I'm just left to imagine
And piece it all together
Makes me yearn for some
One-on-one time with him
To let him be heard
It's been too long
And it's the only lifeline
I have in my toolbox
I pray it's enough
I doubt it's enough
But maybe I'm wrong
I hope I'm wrong

His mom says
She sees a man rising
Out of him
In the aftermath

14. AJ

I ate lunch with him
Took him to Vertigo
And over a burger and fries
He cried and cried and cried

Out of nowhere
Chatting about life and work and
Plans to get ahead
He's always talking about how to dig himself out of poverty
An entrepreneurial spirit
Mind is constantly working

But somewhere in all of that
Talking about his daddy
Exuding joy—he's out of prison
Life has settled into relative security
And the love of his life—
His stability—his friend is home
He shares about the simple pleasures
What his daddy likes to cook for dinner

And somewhere in all that
A pool of tears
From a depth unknown
He sits clearly over his burger
Restaurant sounds all around

Salty water running messy down his face
Just thinking that his daddy could die
Out of nowhere

His daddy is actually fine
But losses of his past haunt him
Stay in his cells
And spill out over lunch

I'm amazed
Saddened
By the sweetness of his love
And his loss
A son wanting to hold his father's hand forever
Dabbing the wound
Dabbing his tears in his soulful eyes
With his greasy napkin

15. JP

Went to bed
And woke up
With that image of you
On my mind

That image of you
Diminished
With Leon County Inmate
Printed across your back

Head down
Shoulders rolled forward
Hands in cuffs
Legs In Shackles
As if you could possibly run

But how does a blind man run?

And I feel angry and sad
But I keep it at bay
If I let this touch my heart
I could die

So I reach for anything
Reach for you dear god

To make sense
To hold on to love

As I want to scream at the judge or the State
You stupid mother fuckers
Your stupid stupid mother fuckers

He's paid the price
Over two years waiting in jail
Guilty until proven guilty
Justice
Protection
A mockery

His sight lost on your time
Lack of care
Lack of protection
Lack of seeing him
A person

Shame on you all for playing god

And will the real God please stand up
I need you to keep this from scarring my heart

As I relive him
Shuffling past his family
Without even a hello
"Happy to see you"
No longer there to him

Tear falling down his mama's eye
Sobs from his little itty bro
As he rides the elevator
Far away from his big bro
"I didn't get to see JP"

And JP
Shoulders slumped
Humanity taken
Never to gaze upon his family again

Dear God take the image from my mind
Or show me how it's meant for love

16. Austin and AJ

What happens when you lose your mom
Lose your world
Snatched away
At such a young age

AJ
Walks stoically
Like a badass
Down the halls of Leon High
But behind closed doors
He cries and cries and cries

Mom dead
Dad—best friend—
In prison
Both gone in one month
A blink of an eye

World smashed in on its head

Angry
Scared
He's walking despair
Trapped in a group home

And he hits a door
Punches all that fear
Frustration and smashes it
Just like his world

ARREST THAT CRIMINAL

Austin
He won't talk (at first)
Mom
His world
Best friend
Closest person
Gone
Gone
Gone

It's been three years now—still
Tears tears tears

How does one cope

How does he keep her close?

"On every sleepless night
I like to drive and drive and drive

On the back country roads
Wakulla
My mama lived there

I take her car
She's close
In the middle of the night—
I drive away
Trying to outrun the grief
Trying to find her
Get close to where I might find what's left"

Too bad I'm underage
Too bad that's too much to explain
When the sirens come on

ARREST THAT CRIMINAL

That's what happens when you lose your mom
Lose your world
Snatched away
At such a young age

I love you both...
Wish I could be your mom...
Take the pain
The tears
Away

17. Jontonia

Fourteen years in a 70-year-old mind
Sometimes
And then her dramas play out as her rightful age

But there is this wisdom
As she grabs her needs sheet
To pay attention to herself
And all that I've taught her

Every week she slows down
Reflecting deeply on her life
And spills all on her heart and mind
With a level of purpose
And focus
And connection
That I can't quite capture in words

She seems to be so much better now
And her family too
As outside influences have minimized
Thanks to COVID
No more fights inside or outside the household
It's quieter there when I call
And quieter in her storytelling

Yet she holds on to the connection teaching NVC
She tells me
Unsolicited
About reaching for empathy—needs inquiry
As she muddles through her 14-year-old love life

Her tellings
Are food for my soul
Hope
That my efforts are not in vain

Peace IS possible
It's in the making
On a timeline
Perhaps different than my own

And she brings me that gift
Hope
As she shares so fully every week
Trying to figure out a new way to move in the world
With compassion

18. Quevon

My miracle
Gift from beyond

My bridge to the other side
With an energy
That captivates
With palpable love
Inquiry
Knowing

How can I ever repay you
For your courage
Willingness to
Jump into the canoe
And paddle to new places

Thank you
For being willing to lean into
The possibility
The unknown

Thank you for taking a hit
For your team
And all of humanity

I love you and I'm in awe of you
I can only sip
The same courage that you display every day

And I pray for ease in your life
As I'm broken and you are whole
Teach me how to stand in such dignity
While standing in the daily uncertainty
Of tomorrow

Standing in daily dignity in a world attempting to diminish your soul

I am the student and you
The teacher

19. Trent

I see you
Everyday
In the ICU
I'm there
In my mind
You are with me every day

There's an indent
Left in my mind
On my heart
Every cell
A sacred calling
To never forget you
Or that moment

I see you
In the ICU
Everyday

Your eyes saying
What your voice cannot
A tube violently stuck in your throat
Tears of joy
Touched
Gratitude
For we have come

To stand by your bedside
Hold your hand
As you struggle to breathe
Senseless bullet lodged in your throat

I've waited six months to capture this moment
To give proper honor to you
A vigil for that time
In the ICU

My heart grabbed and squeezed so tightly
I can't breathe either
Still struggling for oxygen—even now
When I see you in that moment

The smell of scared shit
Coming from your body
A body given over to God
Nauseating to inhale
Embarrassed for your dignity
To be experienced in such a raw state
Vulnerability times 100

And your eyes pleading
Wide open w fear
Tear trickling down
From the corner
Saying
I'm surprised you've come
I'm hurting

I'm sorry I've come to this
I love you all
Thank you for being here

And you keep trying to get the words out
Pe pe pe
Pe pe pe
Shaking your head emphatically yes
When I guess your need
To pee
Yes yes yes
I try to explain about the catheter
You shake your head
No no no
Pe pe pe
Round and round and round
This pseudo conversation goes
A never-ending merry-go-round
As I continue to smell your shit
And love you so fully
Until the nurse comes
Asking us to get off the merry-go-round

And I'm shamefully glad to leave
To escape that strange painful party
Gathered by your bedside
Which I still can't capture adequately
The indent imprinted further
In the silence we held
As we walked
Single file

Out of the ICU
Down the long hospital hall
Back into the world
With new eyes
Never to see the same again

But I see you
Every day
You are with me
Guiding me to a new direction
I'm trusting the path
Trusting I'm not turning away
As much as being guided to a place where I can breathe again
With new lungs
For both of us

I see your mother
Fist held high
Praising god
As we lay you to rest

Trusting
You
Your story

The hospital bed
Bullet
Stench
Tear
Love
They live fully with me now

Every day
I see you
In that ICU
And I remember you
Before too

Make my life
A living monument
A testimony
To the tragedy
Love and joy
And smelly complexity
Of what I took from it all
Propel me into greatness
And help move us all to greater heights

Your legacy
Your indent
Keep it all close to my heart
I want to feel you always

20. Ventavious

Came back
On his own
To volunteer
I tried to lift his 6-foot frame off the ground
Out of excitement
Out of hope
Out of possibility

He came back
I'm guessing
To the place
He FINALLY
Found Connection

Connection
The energy that exists when people experience being seen, heard, and valued
When they can give and receive without judgment

This connection creates safety
Ventavious came back for more

And he handed out the Post-it notes
An offering to help
To be a part
To help create more of this goodness
This safety

A small small act
From someone who came to us lost
Bitter
Scared
Consumed in the smoke he uses to block hell

But we caught it
The staff caught his offering
And tucked it away in our hearts for a day when we need to remember
The power of what we are doing
The power or connection.

Ventavious came back

21. Ron

As the rain comes down
Tears from heaven
I feel the heaviness and beauty of your life

Am I the only one
So dialed into your life
To see all the connections?

Learning to be a trained killer
You laugh when you see
Your fellow soldiers crying
Because of their fear and despair

Learning that it's weakness that will end
With a bullet or a bomb
Tearing your existence to pieces
No space for tears

But your existence
Let's talk about that
Hard to capture in mere words

Dad crazy mean
Due to his own trauma
Due to your granddad's trauma

Thrust on us all
Due to this world's way
Of pitting us against one another
For resources

We all want to feed our families
Have
Rest
Balance
Joy
Been brainwashed to believe
There is scarcity

And that scarcity ends with
A bullet or bomb
Tearing your existence to pieces
Or someone's

I know you
This is your last resort
After all the ongoing trauma
To make yourself secure in this world

What a choice to be brought to

You're perfect fodder

To be shaped into
Someone that can kill and go forth

So much resilience already built into your soul

But I pray—
You don't lose focus
Of the end game
To take your full story
And use it for the good

Which is who you are to me
Nothing but pure good
Saluting to the will
Of what this world has offered you
Thus far

And I know your greatness
And your intellect
And your heart
Even when you lose sight

I see you as a professor
One day
Or a lawyer
Doing the work
So others learn from your existence
Or systems are shaped
Because of your will

And we don't have to train our wounded souls
To go to war
To kill or be killed
Because it's the only choice left

We are better than that

Look around and
See the goodness
In the soldiers sleeping around you

Love surfaces in strange ways
But it surfaces.

Hang on to it

22. Bipolar

I love it
I hate it

I love the people
The hugs
The heart
I love the possibility of hope
Maybe we can move this mountain
Maybe we can make a better world

But maybe there is no better tomorrow
Maybe the better world is now
And being with you
Sharing
Hearing your struggles
Knowing you deeply
Laughing crying

Am I bipolar
Or
Just addicted?

Addicted to your heart
Addicted to the love that shows up in so many forms
Presence practice
Opens the door to leaning in and

Knowing fully
Authenticity
It's addicting

And the people—
They keep coming
Outsiders willing to help
They too get caught in the addiction
We need thousands
Millions of these addicts

And slowly
Surely
They keep coming
And smoke the possibility right along with me

It's what keeps me coming back for more
Even though
My body
And mind
And spirit
Suffer at times—being eaten away by the cancer
Eaten by the violence
Poverty
Imprisonment
Of those I love

I can't help it.
The pull is too strong
All this love

It keeps me going back for one more hit
And when I do—there's no regret
Only the high
Until it wears off
And reality is waiting—

Back and forth
Back and forth

I love it
I hate it

I can't break out of it
Going in circles
Of deep
Amazing love,
Gratitude
Connection
And the despair
Waiting for us—the despair

Going in circles
I love it
I hate it

23. Peeling My Papers

Off the wall
Taped there long ago
Adhesive hanging on them still
Refusing to let go
As I peel myself
From the memories
And love

How many nights did I leave this place
Full
Exhausted
A huge internal smile
Filling me up
Like their love
Their tragedies
Their hope
Connection
And trust

They trusted me
And now I'm gone
Slipped out in pure daylight
During a pandemic
Never to be seen
This departing

I'm grateful not to look them in the eyes
And say goodbye
I don't think they could understand
I can barely make sense myself
How to leave
The ones I love
How to leave
A love I've never known
This deep deep thing

I can't make sense
Yet I do know it's right
And I'm trusting
Through the pain
The loss
I'm trusting

As I step back north side
I carry you with me

Leaving my years of you
In a bag in my car
Not sure what to do with it all
But trusting
It will be revealed

Where to hang
All of those things now?
The letters
The pictures

The love
Loss
Trauma
Death
Learning
Connection

I want to tape you somewhere
Somewhere where everyone can see
And contribute
To your well-being

I won't forget

24. I've Abandoned Ship

The captain jumped overboard
Leaving the crew
And human cargo below
To sail on their own
While I set out for shore
To regain my land legs
And build a
Bigger
Better
Boat

But they follow me
Darn it
They follow me
Right into my dreams
Knocking at my door
At 2:30 in the morn
Waking me up
Grabbing my attention
In the dark of the night

And I sit with them
And my heart and body
Feel the pain
Of their lives
Their existence

Their stories
They haunt me
In the middle of the night
And I let them
I am weirdly grateful
To hold them close

And God continues
To give me strength
To do my part
On land
From the beauty of my own Garden of Eden
Surrounded with
Abundance and love

I'm grateful for
All of it
I wish I could sleep
But know you are waking me
To guide me
My lack of sleep
Is the price I pay
To hold you near
While I live
A blessed and beautiful life
Guilt—
Yes
I wrestle through my war-torn mind

Excited by my soon-to-arrive Dyson Stick
While Jasmine and Ron, Quevon and Tray suffer
The ravages of poverty and systemic racism
And there is little I can do
To clean up their lives

I know it's okay to suck
All of the Schmutz
From every corner of my immediate space
To control what I can
Making beauty in my own backyard
Fortifying me
Giving me someplace
To gaze and revive my soul
While the ghosts of my ship wake me
And ready me for my next journey

Tapping tapping tapping at my soul
I won't forget
I can't forget
The details are fuzzy now
But your energy
Love
Pain
Are imprinted
And move me
To do what I can
Without selling my soul

It's tricky
So tricky
Holding onto my life
While throwing out a lifeline
And keeping
From sinking with the ship
And praying
They don't go under
While I do what I can
Refusing to sacrifice
The only life
I can truly save
My own

25. While We Worry Ourselves about Masks

And the division grows
Righteous Hate settling into our bones
The rest of life does its Thing

Birds singing songs
to greet the day
Teasing breeze
Sweeping into the room—
Saying fall is on the way
Ants crawling on the baseboards—
Marching soldiers
Daring to be
Where they shouldn't

Oh the simplicity
Sometimes
I wish
I didn't think!

Or
Can my mind bring me back
To a place of loving
In spite of
Masks on or masks off?

This is my task
For this lifetime
To take my lessons
By the life
That surrounds me

How lovely that would be!

Appendix B:
Graphics Index

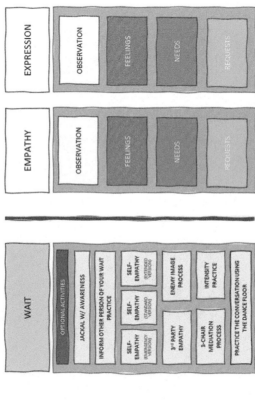

Figure 7: The NVC Dance Floor

...Presence...

EXPRESSION
OBSERVATION · FEELINGS · NEEDS · REQUESTS

EMPATHY
OBSERVATION · FEELINGS · NEEDS · REQUESTS

WAIT

OPTIONAL ACTIVITIES

JACKAL W/ AWARENESS

INFORM OTHER PERSON OF YOUR WAIT PRACTICE

SELF-EMPATHY (EMERGENCY VERSION)

SELF-EMPATHY (STANDARD VERSION)

SELF-EMPATHY (EXTENDED VERSION)

3rd PARTY EMPATHY

ENEMY IMAGE PROCESS

3-CHAIR MEDIATION PROCESS

INTENSITY PRACTICE

PRACTICE THE CONVERSATION USING THE DANCE FLOOR

...Presence...

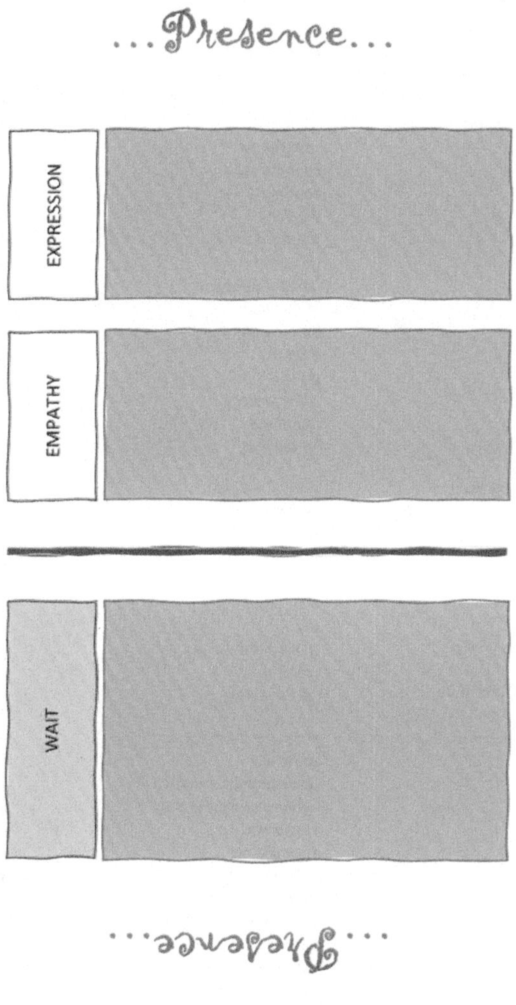

Figure 8: The NVC Dance Floor Simplified

...Presence...

EXPRESSION

EMPATHY

WAIT

...Presence...

Figure 9

UNIVERSAL HUMAN NEEDS

WELL BEING	EXPRESSION	CONNECTION
Sustenance/Health	Autonomy/Authenticity	Love/Caring
abundance, thriving	choice	affection
exercise	congruence	closeness
food/nutrition	consistency	companionship
rest, sleep	continuity	compassion
sustainability	dignity	intimacy
support, help	freedom	kindness
survival	honesty	mattering, importance
wellness	independence	nurturing
	initiative	partnership
Safety/Security	innovation	presence
comfort	integrity	sexual connection
confidence	power	touch
emotional safety	transparency	warmth
familiarity	openness	
order, structure	wholeness	Empathy/Understanding
predictability		awareness
protection from harm	Creativity/Play	clarity
relaxation	adventure	communication
self-esteem	discovery	consideration
shelter	fun	hearing (hear/be heard)
stability	humor	knowing (know/be known)
trust	inspiration	presence
	joy	respect
Peace/Beauty/Rest	movement	seeing (see/be seen)
acceptance	passion	sensitivity
appreciation, gratitude	spontaneity	
awareness		Community/Belonging
balance	Meaning/Contribution	cooperation
clarity	aliveness	equality
ease	achievement, productivity	fellowship
equanimity	celebration/mourning	inclusion
harmony	challenge	interdependence
presence	competence	harmony
recreation	efficacy	mutuality
relaxation	effectiveness	reciprocity
simplicity	feedback	solidarity
space	growth	support
tranquility	learning, clarity	trust
wonder	mystery	
	participation	
	purpose, value	

John Kinyon — www.mediateyourlife.com

Figure 10: Other Conversational Responses

When the other person is in conflict with someone else (not you)...	When the other person is in conflict with someone else or you are in conflict with each other...	When you are in conflict with each other...
We tend to... • Agree • Relate • One up • Devil's advocate • Sympathize • Commiserate • Champion	We tend to... • Give advice • Minimize • Shut down • Joke • Ask questions • Comment • Explain	We tend to... • Threaten other • Correct other • Explain to other • Evaluate other • Criticize other • Blame other

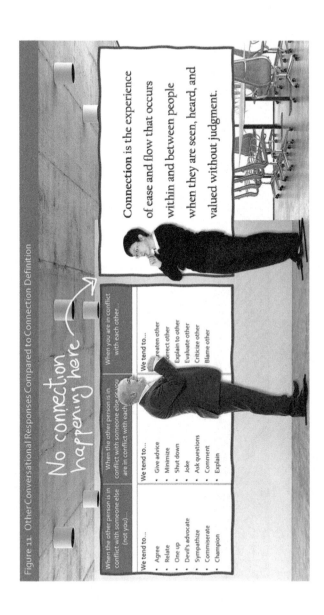

Figure 11: Other Conversational Responses Compared to Connection Definition

No connection happening here

When the other person is in conflict with someone else (not you)…	When the other person is in conflict with someone else or you are in conflict with each…	When you are in conflict with each other…
We tend to…	We tend to…	We tend to…
• Agree	• Give advice	• ...reaten other
• Relate	• Minimize	• ...rrect other
• One up	• Shut down	• Explain to other
• Devil's advocate	• Joke	• Evaluate other
• Sympathize	• Ask questions	• Criticize other
• Commiserate	• Comment	• Blame other
• Champion	• Explain	

Connection is the experience of ease and flow that occurs within and between people when they are seen, heard, and valued without judgment.

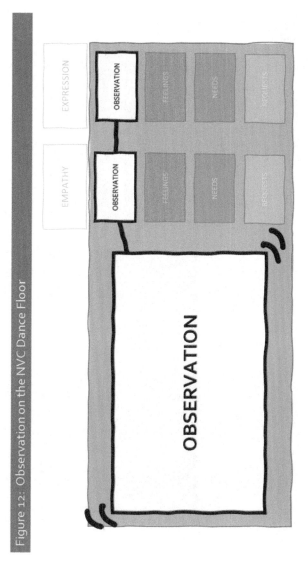

Figure 12: Observation on the NVC Dance Floor

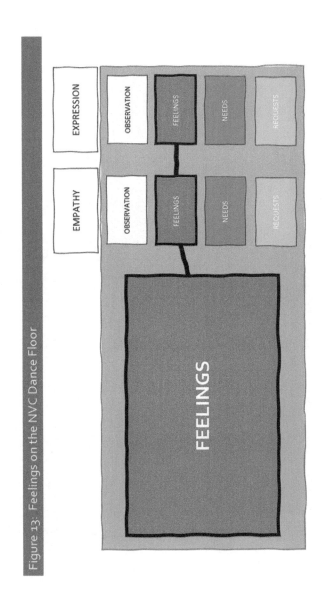

Figure 13: Feelings on the NVC Dance Floor

Figure 14

UNIVERSAL HUMAN FEELINGS

PEACEFUL	LOVING	GLAD	PLAYFUL	INTERESTED
tranquil	warm	happy	energetic	involved
calm	affectionate	excited	effervescent	inquisitive
content	tender	hopeful	invigorated	intense
engrossed	appreciative	joyful	zestful	enriched
absorbed	friendly	satisfied	refreshed	absorbed
expansive	sensitive	delighted	impish	alert
serene	compassionate	encouraged	alive	aroused
loving	grateful	grateful	lively	astonished
blissful	nurtured	confident	exuberant	concerned
satisfied	amorous	inspired	giddy	curious
relaxed	trusting	touched	adventurous	eager
relieved	open	proud	mischievous	enthusiastic
quiet	thankful	exhilarated	jubilant	fascinated
carefree	radiant	ecstatic	goofy	intrigued
composed	adoring	optimistic	buoyant	surprised
fulfilled	passionate	glorious	electrified	helpful

MAD	SAD	SCARED	TIRED	CONFUSED
impatient	lonely	afraid	exhausted	frustrated
pessimistic	heavy	fearful	fatigued	perplexed
disgruntled	troubled	terrified	inert	hesitant
frustrated	helpless	startled	lethargic	troubled
irritable	gloomy	nervous	indifferent	uncomfortable
edgy	overwhelmed	jittery	weary	withdrawn
grouchy	distant	horrified	overwhelmed	apathetic
agitated	despondent	anxious	fidgety	embarrassed
exasperated	discouraged	worried	helpless	hurt
disgusted	distressed	anguished	heavy	uneasy
irked	dismayed	lonely	sleepy	irritated
cantankerous	disheartened	insecure	disinterested	suspicious
animosity	despairing	sensitive	reluctant	unsteady
bitter	sorrowful	shocked	passive	puzzled
rancorous	unhappy	apprehensive	dull	restless
irate, furious	depressed	dread	bored	boggled
angry	blue	jealous	listless	chagrined
hostile	miserable	desperate	blah	unglued
enraged	dejected	suspicious	mopey	detached
violent	melancholy	frightened	comatose	skeptical

John Kinyon – www.mediateyourlife.com

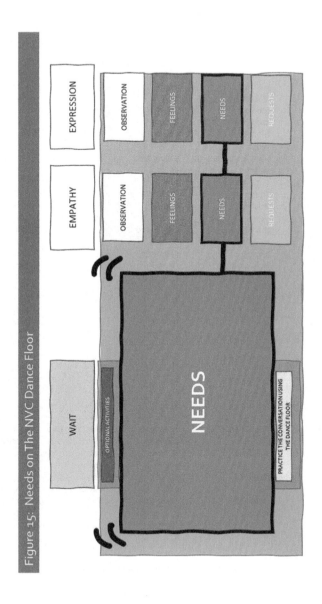

Figure 15: Needs on The NVC Dance Floor

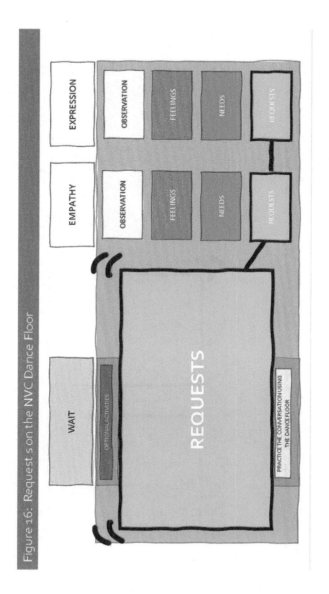

Figure 16: Requests on the NVC Dance Floor

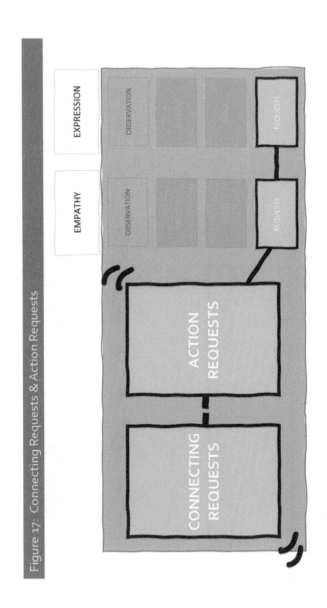

Figure 17: Connecting Requests & Action Requests

Figure 18: Types of Connecting Requests

Request for:	Examples:
1. **Dialogue**	• Can we talk? • Are you open to talking about what happened, now or when you're ready? • Would you like to express yourself first?
2. **Empathy**	**Speaker asks listener to give empathy:** • I'm not sure I was clear. I'm wondering what you heard about my feelings and needs? • It's on me (not you) to be sure I communicated what I wanted you to hear. Would you be willing to tell me what you heard, specifically what I'm feeling and needing? **Listener gives empathy and asks speaker to respond:** • Did I get that right? • Did I understand your needs correctly?
3. **Expression**	**Speaker asks listener to express:** • How was that for you to hear? • After hearing what I shared, I'm curious what's going on for you? What are you feeling, what are you needing? **Listener asks to express:** • Thanks for sharing. Do you mind if I say a few words next? • I'd like to respond to what you just said. Would that be ok?

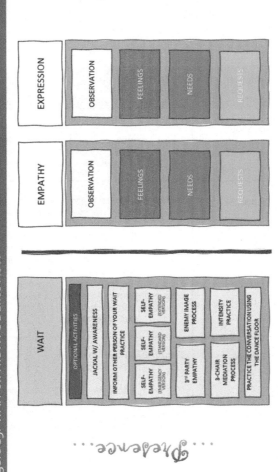

Figure 19: WAIT on The NVC Dance Floor

...Presence...

| EXPRESSION |
| OBSERVATION |
| FEELINGS |
| NEEDS |
| REQUESTS |

| EMPATHY |
| OBSERVATION |
| FEELINGS |
| NEEDS |
| REQUESTS |

| WAIT |
| OPTIONAL ACTIVITIES |
| JACKAL W/ AWARENESS |
| INFORM OTHER PERSON OF YOUR WAIT PRACTICE |
| SELF-EMPATHY (EMERGENCY VERSION) |
| SELF-EMPATHY (STANDARD VERSION) |
| SELF-EMPATHY (EXTENDED VERSION) |
| 3RD PARTY EMPATHY |
| ENEMY IMAGE PROCESS |
| 3-CHAIR MEDIATION PROCESS |
| INTENSITY PRACTICE |
| PRACTICE THE CONVERSATION USING THE DANCE FLOOR |

...Presence...

Appendix C: Recommended Resources

PODCAST

It's All About Connection—NVC with Dr. B! (on Apple and Spotify)

RECOMMENDED BOOKS

Choosing Peace: New Ways to Communicate to Reduce Stress, Create Connection, and Resolve Conflict by Ike K. Lasater and John Kinyon, with Mary Sitze and Julie Stiles

My Grandmother's Hands: Racialized Trauma and the Pathway to Mending Our Hearts and Bodies by Resmaa Menakem

Nonviolent Communication: A Language of Life by Marshall Rosenberg

Peaceable Revolution through Education by Catherine Cadden

The Empathy Factor: Your Competitive Advantage for Personal, Team, and Business Success by Marie Miyashiro

What We Say Matters: Practicing Nonviolent Communication by Judith Hanson Lasater and Ike K. Lasater

Your Resonant Self: Guided Meditations and Exercises to Engage Your Brain's Capacity for Healing by Sarah Peyton

RECOMMENDED WEBSITES

"About the CDC-Kaiser ACE Study," https://www.cdc.gov/violence prevention/aces/about.html

Cindy Bigbie: https://www.thebigbiemethod.com/

Center for Nonviolent Communication: https://www.cnvc.org/

"Fast Facts: Preventing Adverse Childhood Experiences," https://www.cdc.gov/violenceprevention/aces/fastfact.html

NVC Academy: https://nvctraining.com

Mediate Your Life: https://www.mediateyourlife.com/schedule/

Acknowledgments

To you who have helped: I love you to the moon and back!

That is the enormity of the love and appreciation I hold for all the people who have contributed to this body of work and who held me, literally and figuratively, as my mom went from life into the mystery. I have thoughts that I could almost write another book to acknowledge all the people who have helped me and continue to do so—the forms of support have been varied and fortify my belief of the good in this world. Thanks for that above all else.

To all the people who rallied in April and May 2022, as my family was blindsided by my mother's sudden illness and eventual death, thank you. I feel deeply held and loved. My brother, sister, and brother-in-law moved into my house for weeks, and you supported us all. Thank you for the healthy food that showed up daily, fortifying our bodies and spirit. My immediate family had no time or strength to think about food, and I know I would have been weakened without your help. Anne Hempel, I love you for organizing the meals, and thanks to the following folks who brought them: Jill Welch, Kimi Johnson, Jenn Powell, Kate Kile, Kelly McGrath, Denise Hale, Christy Johnson, Anne Hempel, Tamara Weinstein, Dan Kahn, Ida Thompson, Rusty and Laura Payton.

I still can't believe Wil Johnson set up his massage table in the ICU waiting room, stayed for hours into the night, and pulled every inch of stress out of my body—and did the same for my sister too. And that was only the beginning. He came to the hospital a second time and to my house several times to serve us in this way. Thanks to his wife, Christy Johnson, who joined him once to make sure several of my family members could get a massage. Sitting at my mother's side on a soft hospital bed, rubbing and massaging her for hours and weeks on end wreaked havoc on my body. Your touch and talent were a godsend.

Tamara Weinstein, how can I count the ways you showed up for me and my family? Setting up your own massage table in our treehouse and massaging me, my brother and sister. Coming to the hospital late into the night or to our home hospice arrangement to give my mother acupuncture and bodywork and filling the room with essential oils. Thank you for coming to the hospital and sitting with Mom so that I could take a break and walk around the hospital. Thank you for hooking us up with Heather, the hospice nurse, who proved invaluable at the end in keeping Mom's pain at bay! Thank you for finding my mother's cemetery plot; it's perfect. And thank you for being a witness to the beauty of death.

I'm grateful to my friends who showed up to give me empathy when I put out an SOS: Jeremiah Murphy, Deb Hale, Judy Langston. Thank you, Kelly McGrath, for sitting by my mother's bed, being present with her in your sweet way, and honoring the mystery and beauty of her transition process. Thank you, Len Worley, for flying all the way from Ecuador to be with her in her last hours, for bringing love and care and comfort into my home and for all the soulful, helpful words you shared as we laid her to rest. Thank you, Kate Kile and Georgejean Machulis, for putting together the most beautiful last-minute funeral service. I have so much strange comfort about Mom being buried deep in the earth, largely because of the words you spoke as we put her in the ground. I also feel blessed for the Threshold Choir, who sang Mom into heaven, and for my dear friends Keith and Anne Perlman, who witnessed it all.

Thank you to all the many people who showed up at my mother's celebration of life in Hollywood, Florida. I had no idea how many, if any, people would show. I was touched deeply by all who came, from all the parts and generations of her life. Thank you for sharing your love of Marci. Also, I'm grateful for Alyssa Rothman for finding the space at such a last minute.

Thank you, Sheila Mathis and Nicola Roxburgh, for checking in with me almost every day. Thank you, Melinda Person, for listening daily as we have been doing for years.

Thank you, Asia Clark, for helping me change my mother's soiled bed and for sticking that tube in her to keep her from peeing herself. It was a blessing to find a friend working in the hospital who hugged me so deeply, cared for my mother with such love and dignity, and who remains a support by checking in. (Asia was one of my teens at the RJ program years ago. I'm awed to see the circle of love returned to me in this way.) Thank you to all the medical people—you really are heroes. I loved seeing the love that so many of you gave to my mother in her last days. Sandy Bradford, what a gift to find a longtime friend and doctor at Tallahassee Memorial

Hospital. Your friendship, guidance, and medical knowledge were beyond helpful. Thanks for helping us make sense of things as we navigated the trauma and complexity of cancer. Thank you, Bill Thompson, for fitting my mother in to check out the pain in her neck. I am forever awed by your willingness to help my family. Thank you, Big Bend Hospice, for all the support in Mom's final days; I don't think we would have made it without you.

I was moved beyond words when Ron Fairchild, my hairstylist for decades, came to my house to do Mom's hair. He held her head so tenderly and painstakingly, over hours, gave her back her dignity so she could die as the beauty she was.

Thank you, Ryan Bonhardt, for holding down The Bigbie Method, as I was pretty much vacant, and for my facilitators for filling in for me as needed. It was a great gift to be able to let my day job go and be completely present to the only thing that mattered in that moment. I also had so many clients who reached out—thanks for caring.

To my amazing family, holy shit! I don't know many families that could have handled the stress that clobbered us out of nowhere. My husband, my daughters, my brother and sister, brother-in-law, mother-in-law, daughters' boyfriends, nephews. We are so fortunate to be able to work like a symphony. I loved spending the time with you, and experiencing the precious, tender, beautiful, gut-wrenching moments together—even the pain was beautiful with you all by my side.

I fear I may have missed someone or some category. It's been six months since her death, and it seems like a distant dream with the details slipping further away. I pray I don't hurt someone's feelings by forgetting to acknowledge them and that some grace can be extended.

Regarding The Bigbie Method and this book—the body of work I've been dedicated to for a lifetime—again there is so much gratitude to share. I'm so fortunate to have the best husband on the face of the earth. He's always believed in me and has been willing to flow with the waters that lead me. He didn't blink an eye when I left my lucrative program evaluation work to step into the unknown of restorative work and take a pay cut to work at the local RJ program. He didn't worry at all when I left the RJ program and started a company during a pandemic. On and on, he shows his faith in me and the greater good. I'm so blessed to have him by my side.

I have had so many people support this work in big ways, giving time and talent:

Ryan Bonhardt, you came from heaven out of nowhere and have been my right arm in building The Bigbie Method. Thanks for your heart, your care, your brilliance, and your creative mind. I know you sacrifice quite a lot to help me spread this work.

Jeremiah Murphy, how many hours have you put in to be my thought partner? Thank you for being willing to chat with me on so many early mornings and other times as well, to brainstorm and give empathy and guidance. I don't feel lonely in this work, thanks to you. Your enthusiasm, addiction, and deep knowing of this body of work matches my own and keeps me going in the vision to take it to the masses. Also, I would be remiss not to say thanks for the money you gave to help keep TBM going in the early days.

Andrew Miller, you are another person who came from heaven. I remember all our talks and your big push for The Bigbie Method. We wouldn't be here if it were not for you. I love getting on the call and getting a shot in the arm as you pump me up with ideas and vision on how to lead this baby toward adulthood. I know you have spent many hours in service to TBM—thank you.

Denise Hale, my long-time friend. How lucky am I that you also happen to be a fantastic instructional designer. Thank you for having patience with me as we go through every minute detail in developing the TBM instruction to ensure ease of learning. We always knew we had a mission for something good in the world. Thank you for helping me bring it to fruition and for pushing me to try new things.

Jimmy Springston, you came out of nowhere in my life and have been willing to guide me and TBM with so much valuable business information. I get excited just talking with you because I know you understand the potential of this work and share the dream of getting it to many. Thank you, also, for your early investment in the company. You kept us afloat and have given us the ability to keep growing.

Thank you to my facilitators and co-facilitators: Logan Byrd, Jordan Drake, Juliana Rodriguez, Janelle King, Saskiya Fagan, Te'Von Patterson, Dazzerell Grady, and Kate Kile. It's thrilling to see you sharing this work with others and doing so with integrity. It is not lost on me the beauty and struggle of sharing this work while attempting to live it. Thank you, Heather Claypoole, for the delightful experience of sharing NVC via our podcast and helping the work grow an audience.

I'm grateful to all the youth and the community volunteers and staff at the RJ program. I learned so much from you. Mostly my heart is filled and informed by your deep sharing and trust. You have given me profound proof of the value of this work. I am grateful to know you at such a real level, and I am renewed and bigger because of knowing you.

Thank you to anyone who has allowed me to share NVC with you and for being open to receiving. Thank you, Marshall Rosenberg, for developing the model that, I believe, is changing the world for the better, and to the entire NVC community for the shared reality and support around this work.

There were several people who took the time to read this book before it was published and to provide feedback and encouragement: I appreciate your time, Deb Hale, Tamara Weinstein, Hannah Schwadron, and Judy Langston. Also, thank you to Janelle King, Kassie Jones, and Mikolaj Szeptycki for your examples of going north instead of south.

And last, thank you, Mommy, for asking me to write this book. I knew I would, but I appreciated the push!

About the Author

The Bigbie Method was developed by "Dr. B," a.k.a. "America's Communications Coach." Dr. B is a sought-after Nonviolent Communications practitioner, trainer and speaker with years of successful experience working with incarcerated youth. She is also a champion of Restorative Practices, and in 2019 won the Dennis Maloney Award for Youth-Based Community and Restorative Justice Programs.

For twenty-five years, thanks to her PhD in Instructional Design, she traveled the United States and evaluated hundreds of different educational programs. She saw millions of dollars in grant money being used to support these programs in an attempt to advance our educational systems with few long-term results. And time and time again, she returned to the conclusion that our educational system is not advancing because we are overlooking the social-emotional component that is at the base of all. As a result, she has dedicated her career to bringing restorative practices and Nonviolent Communication to all segments of society: individuals, schools, businesses, and nonprofits.

And now she's compiled her twenty-five-plus years of institutional teaching experience into an award-winning approach that you can access any time and from anywhere.

She was inspired to write this book in honor of her mother who passed on May 5, 2022. Dr. B hopes to memorialize her mother and all that was learned through their relationship and the historical trauma passed down and healed as a result of Nonviolent Communication.

Get Involved Using The Bigbie Method

If you want to:

- Experience more connection with friends, relatives, co-workers, students,
- Feel more comfortable approaching hard conversations,
- Proactively resolve difficult workplace, school, or family situations, and
- Help interrupt the cycle of trauma in all areas of our society

Check out The Bigbie Method at
thebigbiemethod.com

or

Enroll in our program at
learn.thebigbiemethod.com

Made in the USA
Coppell, TX
09 June 2023

17885348R00162